GW00858785

The Success Habit

A Journey to Self-Mastery

Robert Herdman

Dedication

To my amazing daughter Katie who is my rock: You have been with me through the ups and the downs: A true honour and privilege to be your father. "Love ya Squillions"

To my adorable son Presley, such a fun and loveable wee character, whom I love so much: "Home Team"

And lastly

To both my deceased parents, Robert and Kathleen

Who whilst on this earth I never took the time to know, but who taught me much more than I ever realised, until now.

I just want to thank you both for everything you did for me over the years.

CONTENTS

Acknowledgements

I want to thank a few people who have been a big factor in the changes in my life. Changes that have led me in the direction and path I am on now and in the completion of this book:

- Jon Solomon, for welcoming me into your world at a time when I needed a direction. Introducing me to personal development and being there in times when I really needed your help, I will always remember.
- Cal Banyan, for starting me on the journey I am on now as a Hypnotist and Success Coach. The quality of your teaching was priceless. 7th Path Self-Hypnosis is still a huge part of my life, ten years on.
- To all the teachers and coaches I have learnt so much from in my journey through the world of personal development over the last ten years.
- Cherie Magee, for taking the time to write the forward of this book.
- Aidan Hughes for painstakingly going through the manuscript of this book, proofreading and editing where necessary.

"And suddenly you know: It's time to start something new and trust the magic of beginnings."

(Meister Eckhart)

Forward

By Cherie Magee

Strategic Coach/Author of 'How Millionaires Do Reality'

If you look up the word 'success' in any dictionary, it will tell you that to succeed is to "fulfill an aim" or to attain the things you want – it is therefore something that we all share the desire of. After all, who doesn't love seeing their dreams manifesting?

So if success is something we crave - Why isn't everyone achieving their best on a daily basis? Is there something missing? The short answer is *yes*. The problem is most definitions of success forget one fundamental yet simplistic thing –Wealth, Success and Achievement will *never* be something you can pull to you from 'out there' without first aligning something you have available to you right now –*your own mind*.

It is the first and only *real* factor in any successful outcome.

You see, achievement is not reliant on external circumstance; it's not that bad upbringing, those mean friends, that outrageous economy that's always collapsing just as you're about to start dinner– it is *easier* than that – it begins within those (often unknown) habitual thoughts you think and the actions that stem from them. Truly, if you learn some *very* basic principles, daily habits and routines – you too can begin to get what you want in life in a consistent, fulfilling and action based way. You can take back control (no matter who you are or what had to happen before you picked up this book) because starting today, you are going to re-learn success in a way that really works and master it for yourself.

What Robert offers to you is this: A no-nonsense plan of action to get you from where you are now to where you really want to be. Whilst the internet, the media and the gurus have complicated success and overwhelmed you with advice (that frankly you have no idea how to put into practice), Robert reminds you that success is actually pretty straightforward and whenever you structure the process and just go back to the basics – it is something that is available to <u>everyone</u>. With his years of research and experience into the human mind, understanding of language patterns, successful hypnosis and clinical psychotherapy, and having helped thousands of clients for many years to overcome those obstacles that frighten them most, Robert offers a much *clearer* path to your dreams.

In this book, he will show you that you don't lack the ingredients for success – you merely lack the *structure*. You'll feel the truth of this when you recall the many times you've had amazing ideas, business plans or dreams that you began to quieten and make excuses for over time, fearing failure and lacking apparent time or resources. You basically saw the barriers and began to give up as we have all done at one point.

Robert knows all about those nasty barriers and while helping you break them down, he will also show you how to structure your day and follow a set of rituals that will develop those good habits that are necessary for consistent results. I have known Robert for some years now; his passion for peak-performance, his skill of entering your world and his experience is hard to match. In fact, he has to be one of the most dedicated, talented hypnotherapists and speakers I have ever met. His realistic and committed manner when it comes people and his understanding of the mindset behind success is second to very few people out there since he is all about *results, results, results*. And we buy these books for that exact reason – we don't care as much about the theory as needing the practice!

This book will give you a clear guideline that you can really use each day to follow Robert's three key principles:

Learning to take full responsibility for 'you'

Renewing your mind on a daily basis

Having a continuous action plan

With these three things you will learn how to actively do, you simply *must* succeed if you follow it correctly. Because when you start from scratch, you renew yourself. So, no matter how desperately you believe that 'you can never have it' – Robert will constantly shake his head and tell you the truth: **You can.**

And by the very last pages of this book, with some mental elbow grease and a really good teacher? **You will.**

Cherie Magee

http://howmillionairesdoreality.com

"The bridge between knowledge and skill is practice,

The bridge between skill and mastery is just time."

(Jim Bouchard)

INTRODUCTION

Mastery

- *The action of mastering a subject or skill*
- *Comprehensive knowledge or skill in a particular subject or activity*

Jesus, The Dalai Llama, Bruce Lee, Richard Branson, Bill Gates, Warren Buffett, Steve Jobs, Tiger Woods, Michael Jordan, Muhammad Ali, Al Pacino, Robert de Niro, Tony Robbins, Paul McKenna; names we would associate as being masters in their given profession or chosen field. Masters are people we look up to, follow, learn from, admire and in many cases idolise. They are people who have "mastered" what they have done and have become household names and icons. But what about you, could you ever consider yourself to be a master at something? Could you be the master of you? This book is all about showing you how to become a master of you, through "self-mastery."

The definitions of "Mastery" above where taken from the Collins American dictionary and the Oxford English dictionary, and when you look at the word in the proper context; self-mastery and becoming a master of what you do is a very basic concept. Through the content of this book I want to show you a way of achieving it.

When I was fifteen years old, I got involved in bodybuilding and over the next ten years I competed at a

National and International level. I competed in twelve bodybuilding competitions over a seven-year period and I placed first in ten of those twelve competitions. I won The Mr.Ireland three times, The Mr N.Ireland three times and The Mr.Ulster twice.

I also competed in the Mr.Britain, where I finished tenth, and I qualified for and also competed in the Jnr Mr.Universe.

So from a very young age I knew what it was like to have self-discipline in my life and this was probably the only thing I was ever passionate about other than what I am doing now. I got up each day and my life was routine. I had a set of rituals that I put into practice every day. Each morning at 5am, I got up had a pre-workout light meal and I went to the gym.

I came home and had breakfast, then went to work (my jobs varied each year but they were just a source to pay for my bodybuilding needs, so the jobs weren't important to me at that time). I came home from work, went back to the gym and finished my day with another two meals and recording what progress I had made each day in my journal. When I look back at what I did then, I would probably consider myself a "master" at what I was doing because it was my life. I was doing the same thing day after day and I was getting, what I thought, were great results and achievements.

Today I am in private practice as a Clinical Hypnotherapist and Success Coach and have been for almost ten years. Over this period of time I have worked with around ten thousand clients, both on a one to one basis and through my seminars and workshops. I have helped clients with many issues over that period of time ranging from abuse, depression, stress, addictions and habit control.

I have developed my own coaching program to help people structure their lives. My past clients have been from all walks of life but over the last few years I have steered my direction from the therapy aspect of my work (even though I still do some) and have focused mainly on coaching; working with people in business and sport.

When working with so many people you get to see that people fall into certain patterns and for a great number of the people who came to see me, there was nothing wrong with them, other than their patterned thinking. The only thing required to help them change their lives was a shift in their thinking and some daily structure to help them break through limiting beliefs and show them a new way to get what they wanted.

Before I became a Hypnotherapist I spent most of my adult life drifting from one thing to the next. I got involved in many businesses and projects with other people but I never really had a focus. I always liked making money and I was always a self-starter but I didn't really know what I wanted or didn't have a passion for anything. I served my time as a French polisher and cabinet maker when I left school, then worked as a barman for a few years. I then worked as a bouncer in various nightclubs around Ireland for around fifteen years. I promoted my own nightclub, owned a beauty and tanning business, owned my own limousine company, bought a van and went to auctions buying old furniture, restored them and resold them. I went into direct sales and worked there for 6 six years, happily but with no real goal. I met a girl who was an amazing singer, so I auditioned a few other singers and started up a band. I did all the promotion and marketing myself and toured around Ireland in pubs and clubs, sitting in the background as a roadie and doing the lighting and sound when they were on stage (I knew nothing about amplifiers or PA's or sound so I just blagged it until I got it right). I was never good at working for other people or taking orders so I really just went through life and if I liked the idea of something I would just do it. I knew very little about most of the businesses I got involved in, I just jumped in with two feet and picked it up as I went along. But all the while there was always something missing.

I never really had a passion for any of these things so I got to a certain stage and then thought" is this it" and then my mind was on something else so I started doing that. Up until I was thirty-five years of age I never knew what the hell I was going to do with my life but I knew there was something I was meant to do. I just didn't know what it was. In 2007, both my parents died of cancer about eight weeks apart and this was such a challenging time for myself and the rest of my family.

I decided to go to California, to distract myself from what had just happened. Back in 2002 I had completed a few certified courses in Neuro Linguistic Programming, for my own personal development, but in September 2007 I saw a training course online to become a certified Clinical Hypnotherapist and Psychotherapist and I thought that this was the perfect opportunity to focus my mind on something while I tried to come to terms with the death of my parents. I didn't have a very good relationship with my father for most of my adult life and my mother's death caused me a lot of heartache, most of which I kept to myself and dealt with in my own way. I have totally come to terms with what happened regarding my parents and I can honestly say that what I have learned through the work that I do as a success coach, I have been able to put into practice what I teach others, allowing me to make peace with both of them in my own self. Over a period of time I was able to let go of all the nonsense within my mind that was holding me back regarding my parents' death, the guilt; the anger and the resentment. I made peace with them and used my skills in Hypnotherapy to develop my Mind-Set to a state of peace and harmony when I thought of them. My time spent with Cal Banyan in California, on his 5-Path Hypnosis training program, would totally change my life. I knew when I was sitting in my hypnotherapy class each day I had found something special that really excited me. This was what I wanted to do with the rest of my life. This twenty-one-day course was nothing like I had ever experienced before. I was hooked. When I got home I immediately searched for suitable premises to set up my own hypnotherapy practice and within two weeks of completing my first certified course in Hypnotherapy, I was in private practice as a Clinical Hypnotherapist and Psychotherapist. I called my clinic *The Belfast Hypnosis Centre* and I still have that practice up and running as I write this book.

Since then I have taken part in a number of training programmes, travelling to different parts of the world to update my knowledge base on personal development and human behavioural change, studying with and having learned from some of the best trainers and coaches in Hypnosis, NLP and Life Coaching.

I can truly say that there has not been one day that I have not love what I am doing. Over the years I have found my niche in what I loved to do within my profession and have found myself really passionate about coaching clients rather than therapy. I help people become successful in different aspects of their life by showing them the key components that they need to put into place in order to make their idea of success become a reality.

Becoming successful at anything in life is simpler than you think. The main reasons people are not successful is more to do with what they are not doing and a lack of certain disciplines. By making a few simple shifts in certain areas, all of a sudden success, in anything, can become a lot more achievable than you think.

I want to use this book as a simple guide to help you put into place a set of principles, that when followed, will help you not only see success in a different way but help you think and act as a successful person even before you have attained your outcome.

I know not everyone reading this book will instantly become successful and I don't expect anything of the sort. If you think about it, if every single person was successful at what they did then success wouldn't really mean that much, as everyone would be doing it. But the truth is, everyone is not successful and there are certain reasons why. I do believe that if everyone reading this book put into practice what is outlined within these pages of this book they would become successful in the manner in which they individually define success. However, I know that only a small percentage of people reading this book will actually follow through and will act accordingly, but these are the ones that I have written this book for.

So please make a decision right now before you get into the content of this book and be a part of that small percentage that will actually embrace the teachings of this book. These teachings are not something I have created, but some of the best philosophies, psychologies and strategies I have gathered from many successful people throughout the world.

I have used these myself and with many of my clients over a ten-year period. When you want to achieve something, in most cases there is no need to reinvent the wheel. Simply find other people who have succeeded in that area before you and model their success, it couldn't be easier.

The only limitation after that are the ones you put up yourself.

This book should be a practical read for you, if you are serious about your success, so it asks you to follow certain practical exercises at the end of each chapter to help you develop a structure and weed out some of the things that may be holding you back.

So before we start I want to give you your first practical task;

One of the most important things that I have used throughout my life is a journal. I have been using a journal from I was fifteen and I didn't even know what I was doing. I just knew at that time it helped me to record what I had done on a daily basis regarding my bodybuilding career so that I could look back and reflect on my success and also change the things that didn't go according to plan. A journal is simply a reflection of your daily activities. It's part of a game plan that will help you get some structure into your life. It helps you develop a structure for your success and acts as a platform and a guide of your progress. It also helps you get all the crap out of your system by writing it down.

Once you can identify all the negative stuff that has been going around your mind and get it out of your head and onto paper, you can see all the stuff you don't like and don't want. So now you can see what you need to get rid of.

When you have too much racing through your mind it can drive you mad, and you start to focus on things that aren't important and it's easy to get lost. On the other hand, when you wake up each morning and you have a plan right in front of you, in your journal, then it's simple; you just check the list off as you go through the day. Each day that passes you find yourself getting closer to your goals by practical application "Simples" (I will cover this in more detail as we go through the chapters).

So before you turn the page I ask you to get yourself your very own journal and use it as you go through this book. Remember this is a practical book and requires you to actually "Do Stuff" and get involved in your own success.

So once you have your own journal, get yourself into a comfortable position and "Let's begin a new journey together" ….

The world we are experiencing today is a result of our creative consciousness,

And if we want a new world, each of us must start taking responsibility for helping create it."

(Rosemary Fillmore Rhea)

Part 1

Taking
Responsibility
For
You're Life

"You'll either pay the price of success or the price of regret.
The price of success weighs ounces.
The price of regret weighs tons.
It's Your Choice."

(Ruben Gonzalez, Three-time Olympian)

1

WHAT DOES SUCCESS MEAN TO YOU?

"Would you tell me, please, which way I ought to go from here?"
"That depends a good deal on where you want to get to."
"Oh I don't much care where- "
"Then it doesn't matter which way you go"
(-Lewis Carroll, Alice in Wonderland)

You did get a journal right? Good, just checking.

Why is it that some people succeed while others can barely make it through life?

How can one individual become a massive success in their business or sporting career whilst tens of others, with the same ability and talent struggle or fail miserably?

Why do successful people always seem to move forward, no matter what the economy or the circumstances, whilst the majority of people stumble at every hurdle?

Successful people have the same challenges on a daily basis as everyone else. They have the same bad days; the days when they want to give up and the days where nothing seems to be going right.

Most importantly they have the same 24 hours in a day that everyone else has. Their lives are just as busy, from they get up in the morning until they go to bed at night, sometimes even more so. So why do they become successful whilst the majority of people don't or simply just get by in life?

In studying successful people and their habits, I believe that there are a series of commonalities that contribute to their success.

What I have learned over the years is that being successful at anything in life is not an accident it is a very deliberate and systematic feat. Throughout the pages of this book my aim is to share with you a way of thinking and doing, that can help you become successful. But first of all let me ask you a more direct question.

What does success mean to you? I mean, really and truly, what would have to happen in your life or what would you have to have or be, to consider yourself as successful?

When we think of it in a general term we tend to associate the word "Success" in the eyes of society, as being one large achievement or a final destination that is usually only achieved by top sports people or business men and women or performers. We think of the word success as being prestige and look up to those who have achieved it. They become icons and heroes and the word then fits into a category only designed for the elite, the gifted or the lucky ones.

But the truth is that success means something different to everyone and can be achieved by everyone. Being successful in life is actually a lot simpler than you think. It is there for everyone to experience, with no exception, and is within everyone's grasp when they follow a simple process. When you think about it, you are already successful in life and have already achieved many things in your life.

In this book I want to share with you three fundamental principles that will help you to become more successful in "YOUR" life, no matter what success means to you. Three fundamental principles that if you follow, can change your entire world and your future. Now I know that may seem a bold statement to make, but the reason I believe I have the authority to say such a thing is that I am going to share with you a system I have put into my own life that has helped me literally turn my life around.

I truly believe that if I can do it then anyone can, when they go through a simple process on a daily basis.

The Process of Success

I'm sure as you read this book you will agree with me that everyone in life would love to be successful at something. Whether it's becoming a more successful parent, losing weight, stopping smoking, having a successful career, relationship, business, becoming financially successful, the list goes on and is different depending on the individual.

As a therapist and coach, I have worked with many people from all walks of life and when I have asked each of them the question, "Do you want to be successful?" I can honestly say that not one of them in ten years has ever said no. but their idea of success is personal to them.

So my question to you is this:

Why is everyone not successful? I mean, if this is what everyone wants, even though it means something different to each individual, then why so many people go through life not achieve the success they want, even in the simplest things in their life. This is how I see it.

People love to get results in life; they want for change to happen in their lives and ultimately become more successful at something. However, many times they neglect the recipe that is behind that change taking place and that is **"The Process"**

There is a process to follow in everything we do in life and when you follow the process, that is when things start to happen in your life and if you don't follow the process, then you don't get the results. It is that simple.

Take successful people in any profession for instance: The lawyer studies and practices law on a daily basis to be successful in his profession: he follows a process. The doctor studies and practices medicine on a daily basis to become successful at what she does: she follows a process. An athlete first studies then practices his/her craft on a daily basis to become a champion: they follow a process. But when most people want to change an area of their life they try something once or twice and then if that doesn't work they move onto something else and then something further. It's never their fault; they blame other things, other people or they develop a story and that story becomes their platform which they regurgitate consistently to justify why they have not succeeded.

As human beings we are creatures of habit. We create a habit and through repetition, that habit creates what we will do or won't do. The difference between successful people and unsuccessful people is simply in the difference of their habits. Successful people develop good habits and unsuccessful people develop bad habits, both live by those habits on a daily basis.

For things to change in your life: You have to change, and that means getting rid of some old habits that have been stopping you from becoming successful and developing some new habits that will take you in the direction of the success you want to achieve. And these new habits will require you to do a few things that not everyone is prepared to do such as self-discipline, commitment, diligence, taking responsibility, and a continuous daily effort.

In my profession I get the pleasure to work with a wide variety of people from different backgrounds and ultimately they all want the same thing; to be successful. No matter whether I am working with a top athlete, business person, a housewife, a teenager, I use the same set of principles to help them to achieve success, the same set of principles that I am going to share with you in this book. And furthermore, if you follow these principles, you will be successful at whatever it is you want to achieve, even though I don't know you, I've never met you and I don't even know what it is you want.

But let me first make this clear. Even though I have said on a few occasions in this chapter that success is simple, I do not want to mislead you in anyway by having you believe that this journey is easy, because it's not. Having a goal and accomplishing that goal can be a simple process but it's by no means an easy process.

You're going to have to be prepared to step up to the mark and do some things that you haven't done before. Challenge some of those old beliefs and develop new ones, which can be challenging in itself. Do some things you don't want to do to get you started.

When I work with clients on a daily basis I am quite frank and straight to the point as I will be in this book with you. I believe it is the only way to get lasting change and it separates people into two categories; the ones who really want success and are prepared to do whatever it takes and the ones who would only "like" to be successful. We all have a list of things we would like to have in life but that doesn't mean anything until we are prepared to do what's necessary to turn that "like" into a reality, by implementing a structure, both mental and physically, for that success to occur in your life.

John's Story

John was a 22-year-old man who had been recommended to me by his friend, who had also come to me for help. As John sat in front of me I asked him what I could do for him and his answer was to become successful. I asked him to elaborate and tell me what that meant to him and he spent the next 10 minutes telling me of everything that he didn't want and how much of a failure he considered himself to be in everything that he did. I asked him to be specific on what it was he thought I could do for him and his answer was, "just work your magic on me, help me like you helped Mervin (his friend) because he is doing amazing."

I then proceeded to ask him what success meant to him, and if I could just wave a magic wand and could, "work my magic" as he put it, what would have to happen for him to be successful. His response was a familiar comment that I receive a lot when working with clients and that was, "I'm not too sure, I don't really know but I know I hate my life and I'm totally unsuccessful right now at everything I do." He then proceeded once again to tell me everything he didn't want and didn't have in his life.

"How can I help you become successful if you don't know what success means to you? If you don't know what you want, I can't help you." I told him to his dislike.

After a short period of time we decided to go through a few coaching sessions and I helped him define what success meant to him and develop a plan as to how he could achieve it. The difference between him and his friend was that when Mervin came to see me he had a goal. He knew what he wanted and was just looking some help in implementing a plan to assist him in getting there. John didn't know what he wanted so we had to start from the beginning. Once we developed a blueprint of what he really wanted, and not what he thought he should have; he now had a structure, a purpose and a plan to make his life successful on his terms.

So before we get into the first fundamental principle of success, let me start as I mean to go on.

A lot of people are not successful in life, not because they don't have the ability or talent to be successful, but because they are just too lazy to become successful. They want change to happen in their lives right now, with as little effort as possible on their part. They want to get a hundred percent return but are only willing to put in one or two percent (if even that).

They want to do this over and over again, constantly moving from one thing to the next with no commitment on their part. They want, what I call, **"The magic wand treatment."**

Their attitude being; wave your magic wand and fix me, make me successful, make me slimmer, take away my depression, make me financially independent, but make sure there's no effort on my part. If you are reading this book and this is what you are expecting, then this book is not for you. This is not a quick fix or an easy, no effort, manual for success because I don't believe there is one. However, I do believe that when you are prepared to follow a daily structure, backed with by discipline and commitment then success can be achieved by anyone.

But like everything else in life, this book will only work for you if you actually put it into practice, if you follow the process and practically do the exercises outlined in the following chapters. It will not work if you simply just read it as a novel and toss it aside without application and sit on your backside and wait for "The Universe" to magically create it for you. Knowledge is not power my friend.

It is simply potential power and a mind full of updated knowledge without application is merely an accumulation of information without a purpose. You can have the best strategy in the world for something but if it is not put into practice then it is simply information and that's all.

It doesn't achieve much except maybe make you feel better because you know more.

"Accumulated knowledge put into practice, however, creates miracles."

As a Clinical Hypnotherapist, and Success Coach for just coming ten years now, I have spent a lot of time in private practice helping over ten thousand clients refocus their lives by implementing a simple formula that I have fine-tuned over the years to help people become successful, handling their problems and challenges differently. But wanting to change is simply not enough, knowing how to change isn't enough. Getting motivated isn't even enough for lasting change to take place in your life.

This book is not about getting you all pumped up and motivated. We can all get motivated when we want to, but motivation doesn't last. Seminars and conferences designed to get people motivated work in the moment and can sustain that motivation for about forty-eight hours. But in most cases, a week or two later, that same motivated person has went right back to where they started because they have got back into their old ways and old patterns of thinking and behaving. This is where conditioning comes in; taking a proven system or set or principles that have worked over and over again for many people, and through repetition implementing these principles into practice over a sustained period of time until they become habit. To do this takes discipline, consistency, diligence and developing an unstoppable Mind-Set. So to make this happen in your life you have to be willing to pay the price for success.

There is a price to pay for everything we do in life, whether it be negative or positive, and becoming successful is no different. There is a price to pay for success and there is also a price to pay for failure and in for staying the same, not taking action and achieving your goals in life. We all have the ability to turn our lives around, whether you will or not, that is the question. The things that are simple to do are also easy not to do and when we get into a habit of "not doing," we pay that price for failure and success passes us by. Either you keep paying the price on a daily basis for your past mistakes and bad decisions or you reap the benefits for accepting responsibility for your life. You learn the skills you need to make your life more fulfilling and achieving your goals.

We all have 24 hours in a day that we can choose to use how we wish and achieving a goal takes a lot of time and effort.

The question is what are you going to do with your time? How will you spend each day from when you get up in the morning until you go to bed at night?

How you decide to use those twenty-four hours will determine how successful you will be.

If you're not where you want to be in life or you don't have what you want, it has nothing to do with your past, it has nothing to do with other people's opinion of you or what they did to you, it has nothing to do with the system.

It has everything to do with the fact that up until this present time you have not made the sacrifice and put in the discipline needed to achieve that success. And that is the price you must pay if you want that success in the future.

Remember the only limitations are in your mind, but the great thing about your mind is it can be trained, through repetition, to give you what you want. It's your mind, it's there to be successful and can be adjusted when you follow the right process, and the process, that I will show you later in this book. So let me ask you this question:

For every promise you make yourself, there is a price to pay.

Are you willing to pay the price for success, with no conditions?

If so, then let's get started. All I ask of you are three things:

- *You start at the beginning and open up your mind to the content of this book. For this I ask you to put your old beliefs on hold and not only read the content of this book but act as if it were true. (If what I am saying throughout this book doesn't resonate with you, then you can always go back to your old ways when you have finished. If you take the time to read the entirety of this book, I don't believe this will happen).*
- *You take part in the practical exercises at the end of each chapter that are designed to help you reignite your imagination and re-train your sub-conscious mind.*

- *Start this book with a specific goal or area of your life that you want to change and become successful at. As you read the book and go through the practical exercises you know your purpose and what you want to achieve.*

Remember being successful means something different to everyone and I believe that everyone reading this book will have some area of their life they want to improve or a special goal they would like to achieve, so read this book with your outcome in mind.

If you don't have a goal in mind, how can you achieve it?

In the chapter on goal setting I will help you refine your goals and maybe even help you set new ones. I want you to leave this book embarking on a new journey with a game plan and a practical way to implement that game plan each day. I want you to become a person of action.

To get the most out of this book you have to first define what success means to you and what you would like to achieve. If I could help you become more successful in your life, you have to pinpoint what would have to happen for you to consider yourself successful.

Maybe you are successful in different aspects of your life and are looking for focus on a specific area. Maybe you are looking to transform your life and become successful in many areas.

You could implement the strategies within this book into a few different areas of your life.

Whatever you have in mind, you must first make it clear what success is for you and how you will use the content of this book.

So to finish off this first chapter, let's start off with a quick and simple exercise to make this book more personal to you.

As you read through each chapter you are going to associate your own wants and needs with what you would like to get out of this book.

To be successful in any endeavour the first thing we need to do is to identify our own definition of what personal success in that area would mean. Your pattern of achievement will then follow your definition. So let's start there.

Below I have enclosed a list of questions for you to answer. Time to get out that journal we discussed in the introduction and a pen. As you go through the first exercise of the book I want you to write out the questions in your journal and after each question answer them as honestly and as accurately as you can. The idea here is not to write down something that is going to make you feel great about yourself; it is about the honest truth. At this stage it's not important if you don't like the answers you have written. The truth about where you are right now being more important. Once you are totally honest with yourself you can start to develop the strategies and skills to turn your life around.

The great thing about doing this simple exercise and having your own personal journal is that you will look back on this in a few months' time and see how much your life has transformed in such a short space of time.

Answering these questions honestly will give you an idea of where you are at right now.

Exercise 1: Your Definition of Success.

Write down the answers to each question in your journal

Think about yourself ten or twenty years ago. What was your definition of success back then?

What did you want back then?

What did you think you had to do, be and have in order to call yourself successful?

How close are you to that definition today? Have you achieved it?

What is your definition of success today? Has it changed?

Why has it changed? Have you settled for less than you wanted ten years ago?

What will you have to do, be and have in order to call yourself successful by the end of this year? In five years? In ten years?

If you have not achieved it, what is stopping you from achieving it?

What would you like to focus on as you go through this book? What things are you looking to change in your life?

Are you willing to pay the price to turn your life around?

And lastly, and probably the most important question in this exercise:

What are your reasons for wanting to become successful in these areas of your life? Write down a list of your "Why's"

At this stage of our journey I want you to simply get an idea of what you will focus on and what success means to you. Later in chapter 6, I will go through a very in-depth goal setting exercise that will help you focus your mind better and by the end of that chapter you will have come up with specific goals that you will work on over the next few years.

So let's get moving and onto the first fundamental principle of success, which is the basis of part one of this book.

"Obstacles can't stop you. Problems can't stop you. Most of all, other people can't stop you. Only you can stop you."

(Jeoffrey Gitomer)

2

What's Stopping You from Having An Amazing Life?

"Nothing happens in your life until you get rid of your excuses, get up off your ass and go make it happen, there are no exceptions"

(Robert Herdman)

If you want to become successful in a certain area of your life, then you have to make certain changes for that success to take place. The first thing you must do and I emphasise must do, for lasting success to take place in your life, is that you have got to accept and take full responsibility for your own life. It's your life, no one else's. What that means that what happens to you on a daily basis, is a result of what you allow to keep happening to you on a daily basis.

Many people can barely make it through life; paralysed by their feelings and waiting for their emotions to change before they even attempt to face life. They become what I call "Success Victims," a product of their past failures and masters of, "why they can't" or "maybe someday" or "when things get better for me, then I'll change." The storyteller of their mind dominates their thoughts and they allow their days to be filled with fears, insecurities and excuses. Their mind becomes their enemy and they continually program themselves with self-defeating, self-immobilising data and information, that in turn affects their behaviours on a daily basis. They blame other people for their failures with rehearsed justifications of why they are the way they are.

"If only I had got the breaks in life"

"If I had been pushed by my parents when I was growing up"

"If I lived in a different part of the world then things would be different for me."

And so it goes, a self-fulfilling barrage of thoughts that keep them stuck in mediocre and poverty.

As human beings we can program the most non-seneschal data into our minds that ultimately stops us from achieving what we want to achieve in life. Your mind can think of all sorts of stuff; your mind can get as good as it wants or as nasty as it wants. Your mind can do whatever it wants to do: **If You Let it.**

Taking responsibility for your life means taking back control because when you are in control of your life, everything is different. Now if you're not in control then someone or something else is. But when you make the decision to take back control, then you also decide what your life will be about, and that is such an amazing feeling.

Think about this question for a moment:

What would you do if failure was not an option? If success was inevitable, then what would you want to achieve, be, have or become?

So, let me ask you another question:

What is stopping you from achieving that success?

Because until you find out what is stopping you, you are not in a position to move in the direction that you want to go.

Teresa's Story

Teresa came to see me wanting to lose weight. She was a middle aged woman of around forty-five and she was about five stone over weight. We talked for a few moments about the weight loss program I offered and how it could help her and then I asked her why she was overweight. She told me she was a comfort eater and ate when she was happy, stressed, and sad. She told me her story of how when she was young she had always been made fun of by her mum and sisters because she was a "chubby child." Her way of handling that was to secretly eat when no one was looking. Throughout her adult life she had an older sister who always teased her about her weight and made a point to comment on how she loved food when they were in the company of others. Both her mother and older sister had passed away a few years before she came to see me but she was still using her past and the opinion of others to control her relationship around food. I helped her to start to believe in herself and focus on "Now." I helped her change her relationship with food, helping her take back control of food, instead of letting food and circumstances, control her behaviours around food. She was the only one responsible for herself being overweight and until she actually accepted that, only then could she change it…and she did.

So what stops people from being in control of their lives and achieving the things they really want to?

Let's have a look at a few of the things that stop many people moving forward in life. I'm going to touch on them very briefly so that we can first identify how similar we all can be, but I will not go into detail as this is a book about getting what you want in life, not dwelling on what's stopping you.

The Past

One of the major things that stop people from moving forward in life is being caught up in the past. When we go through life, we go through a lot of experiences; some good and some not so good. But every experience carries with it emotional content and that emotional content is stored within the sub-conscious mind. If we have had a lot of negative experiences that are interrelated, e.g. trying to lose weight many times and failing or being in a series of bad relationships, then even though the experiences come and go, the emotional content of each bad experience becomes stored in the subconscious. It has a compounding effect when faced with new situations involving similar content. We then go through what I call "Emotional Resonance" which means that the memories and emotions of those past events are activated, bringing up the same emotional content when faced with similar experiences. This in turn can stop us from even trying or can lead to self-sabotage. The great thing about the past is that it's over, it doesn't exist anymore.

But what keeps people contained in the past? They keep replaying the memories of past experiencing in their mind, over and over, keeping them contained in those negative emotions. Memories are not real, they are just thoughts, ways of processing information and using your imagination. So taking responsibility for your life means letting go of the past and creating an amazing future for yourself and the people around you, by focusing on "NOW" which is all we have.

Other People's Opinion

Many people will not even attempt to try new things in life because of the opinion of other people. They live in a world where other people's opinion of them actually means more than their opinion of themselves. This paralyses them into a state of mediocrity and silent desperation. This used to be a big controlling factor for me in my life and really effected what I would and wouldn't do. Even as I was experiencing my first years in Private Practice as a clinical hypnotherapist, I was constantly focusing on other people's opinion of how good a service I could provide. This, I realise was stopping me from being the best therapist I could be and it wasn't until I released these old beliefs, that I was able to experience the success I do now with my clients.

What I have found to be true with regards to other people is this:

People are always going to have an opinion no

matter what, because that's the nature of human beings. But the truth is that another person's opinion of you, does not validate who you are as a person and what you can do in life.

I have adopted a philosophy that I have mastered over the last few years, which is this,

"Another person's opinion of me is none of my business so I don't get physically or emotionally involved in it"

As a Hypnotherapist, Coach and Speaker, I have too much to be getting on with in my life to focus on something that I have no control over.

So if this is a big factor for you, your first step in taking responsibility of your life could simply mean adopting this new philosophy. What I did was to learn the above phrase off by heart and I repeated it to myself over and over again. I then found when I was faced with a situation when someone gave a negative opinion of myself or what I was doing, I found this phrase automatically coming into my mind and it stopped me from dwelling on that opinion, which I had no control of, and I simply moved on. It was like a magic switch inside my mind that was always ready and waiting and fired off every time. This became a habit and it now runs on auto-pilot-simple but highly effective. The great thing about this simple technique is that it is universal and will work for everyone, when rehearsed and impressed upon your sub-conscious mind. When you let other people's opinions immobilise you in life, what you are really saying to yourself is that this person's opinion of me is more important than my opinion of myself. This is simply not true. An opinion from someone else should be something you are able to take or leave without allowing it to affect you in a negative way.

The Blame Game

Another controlling factor for many people, that stops them form breaking out and becoming successful, is what I call the "Blame Game".

It's easy to blame other people or circumstances for the things that you don't have in your life and many people live their lives in just that way.

"The reason why I am the way I am is because……"

I'm sure you can think of endless ways to finish this sentence that could put the blame on other things, circumstances or people.

But internally if you are blaming other things for your short comings then you're not in control and therefore do not have the power to change things.

When you are pointing the finger at someone or

something else to attach blame, always remember there are three fingers pointing right back at you.

Where you are in your life right now is no one else's fault. You are where you are because of the decisions and choices you have made in the past. Where you will end up in five or ten years' time is a result of the decisions and choices you make right now, at this present time in your life.

This can be a very hard concept for people to digest, but it's true. I'm not suggesting that if something bad happened to you in the past or someone treated you in a certain way that was unjust, you are to blame. That's not what I'm saying by any means.

What I am saying is that the past is the past, it's over and the events cannot be different, but you have already paid the price for it once. Why would you continue to let those events or people live rent free in your head each and every single day? The only person that is hurting is yourself and by continually focusing on that, you are stopping yourself from moving forward.

A simple decision to move on from the blame game in your life can open up many doors and point you in the direction of endless new opportunities. I will touch on this a bit later and show you a few ways of re-training your mind to let go and free up that energy to put into something more worthwhile.

Excuses

What dreams did you have for yourself as an adult when you were younger? Do you still have those dreams?

Are you moving toward them each day? Or have you replaced them with a list of excuses as to why you cannot achieve them?

As an adult I think over time, I have made every excuse I could think of over the years. I got to the stage where I was sick and tired of being sick and tired. I realised that the only limitations I really had for not achieving what I wanted in my life, was in my mind. So I set out on the goal of re-training my mind to develop a belief, have faith in myself and ignite that inner confidence of myself. I would take small steps each day and just get out there and go for what I really wanted. I don't believe in excuses and I firmly believe if you want something badly enough you will find a way. One of the best pieces of advice I was given was this:

"There are only obstacles or excuses in life. If it's an obstacle, then there will always be a way through it if you're committed. If it's an excuse, then there will always be a hundred more waiting to stop you from being successful."

What are some of the excuses you have been using that are stopping you from experiencing the life you really want?

"I'm too old."

"I'm too young."

"Don't have the talent."

"If only I lived in a different part of the world."

"If I had been pushed more by my parents when I was younger."

"If it wasn't for the economy."

"Not smart enough."

"Don't have a degree."

"Tried before and failed."

"My circumstances."

"Someone else's fault." etc.

Taking responsibility for your life means getting rid of all your excuses and starting with a blank canvas. In psychology this is termed as "tabula rasa," meaning blank slate.

Making the decision to get rid of old limiting beliefs and starting with a blank slate in creating the life you want. It will help you become the person you need to become along the way to the achievement of your goals in life.

FEAR

I would say that this is the most common and most powerful obstacle that holds people back in life. Fear falls into many categories and can literally paralyse and immobilise people, corporations and even countries.

Fear comes in many forms and can be labelled in many ways:

Fear of Failure

Fear of success

Fear of the unknown

Fear of what other people might think

Fear of rejection

Fear of disappointment

Fear of being alone

Fear of commitment

Once again I'm sure as you read this; you could add many others to the list.

So as this is a "biggie." I have dedicated a full chapter on it later in this book, showing you ways of how to embrace it, reframe it and move beyond it. Fear is not real; it is simply a way of processing thought and then acting out on it as if it were real. Fear is an illusion. So I will return to this in more detail later in the book.

Our Life Script

When an actor gets a part for a role in a movie or a play, he is given a script. He reads through the script and familiarises himself with the role and then acts out accordingly. The same is true with us as human beings. Let me explain. Metaphorically when we were younger we were handed a script by our parents, our peers, our teachers and all the other people in our lives that had influence over us and society in general. That script is your reference manual for all the things that you believe to be true about yourself. If you have been programming yourself to believe you're not a confident person, then this becomes part of your life script. When situations come into your life where you need confidence then you refer to your internal script. Confidence is not part of your programming so you allow opportunities to pass you by. As you were growing up, maybe you were taught to play it safe and not take many risks in life. Then once again when an opportunity arises, which requires some level of risk taking on your part, your script tells you to avoid that risk and the chances are you let that opportunity pass by. You will use one of the excuses you have as a backup plan, to justify your decision.

What I am here to tell you is that your life script is not an accurate reflection of who you really are. You are so much more. This book is about rewriting a new script for yourself; taking the things on your old script that don't serve you well and helping you to form new ideals. New beliefs, new learning's, new knowing's. It's about going into the world with a new attitude, a different perspective and mostly a new understanding of who you are and therefore what you are really capable of achieving.

The Story Teller

The story teller is that inner voice which is continuously working inside your mind chatting away narrating your life on a daily basis. That storyteller can be your best friend or your worst enemy depending on what you face in life. It can tell you how great things are and can motivate you to get up and go. Or it can tell you how it's impossible to do things or that you don't have what it takes to face a certain situation. It can put you down and make you feel less than what you are or it can give you a boost and make you feel amazing.

Most people have a story of why they can't achieve what they want to achieve. They tell themselves that story over and over again continually reinforcing their limitation, inabilities and short comings that in turn becomes a belief.

The thing about the story and the storyteller is this; it's not real, we make it up. It's just a series of thoughts we have been telling ourselves that once again has become our reality. But the great thing about your mind is that you can always make up something different and even better.

I believe that if you're going to make something up, then why not make up something that will empower you and therefore tell yourself a different story. And just as with the old story, once you get the storyteller to practice telling you a new story every day, internally over and over again, then that too will become your reality. If you have the ability to make stuff up that really can affect your life, then start making up good stuff. Have that story teller in your mind create the most amazing stories for you filled with success, happiness, and things that make you feel good. It's your imagination. Start having it work for you, instead of against you.

Erroneous Emotions

As human beings we are all emotional creatures, continuously moving from one emotion to another. One day we can feel on top of the world and the next, without warning, we feel as if the world is against us.

As we go through life we can attach certain emotions to certain situations from the past or with people. Some of these emotions can make us feel negative. When we think of that past situation or person, just like a switch, the emotion comes up and this can affect us instantly. These negative emotions can then get anchored into our sub-conscious mind and run automatically below our level of consciousness.

It's when we harbour emotions such as anger, frustration, hate, resentment, worry, guilt, inadequacy and such like, that we find ourselves getting caught up in those feelings. If this lingers within our consciousness, then this obviously has an effect on our daily activity.

Everything we do in life takes energy and when you dominate your thoughts with your erroneous emotions, this wasted energy can make you feel burnt out at the end of each day.

How many people reading this can relate to this?

Imagine if you freed up that energy and put it into something different such as a goal you wanted to achieve, immersing your thoughts in the achievement of that goal. How different could your life be?

Later in this book I will show you some simple techniques to help you overcome these negative emotions so that you can of take back control of your emotional state.

Remember, whatever you allow to happen in your life is ultimately what will continue to happen in your life. If you continue to allow yourself to be a victim of your past and your circumstances, then that's what will continue. If you continue to let your fears and insecurities control or even paralyse you, that's what will continue. If you continue to let the opinions of other people frame your thinking, that's what will continue. Again, the truth is, whatever you allow to happen is what will ultimately persist.

Now if you can resonate with any of the content in this chapter so far, let me ask you a couple of questions:

Are you not sick and tired of how this makes you feel on a daily basis?

Is it not time to stand up for yourself and start doing something different that will help you create a more empowering and fulfilling life?

There are many things that can stop people from moving forward in life. I have outlined a few that in my experience, usually play a large part in the majority of lives. Other problems may be:

Social media Junkie: This has become a new time stealer over the last ten years. Time is the 'stuff' of life and if we allow different things to suck up our time, we are killing opportunity. Sitting on Facebook or other social media sites for hours looking and reading about nonsense, is achieving exactly what it says on the tin, "nothing."

Too many distractions: A lot of people major in minor things and don't prioritise what are the key elements that they should be focusing on, in relation to their goals and achieving them.

Lack of Vision or Purpose: When clients come to see me and I ask them they see themselves in a one year's time, most people haven't a clue. They don't have a vision of what they want their lives to be. When we have a sense of purpose and direction, the distractions become a lot less appealing.

Spending time with the wrong people: It's really simple; if you're hanging out with people who don't push you – you're losing. You're losing out on all the positive relationships you could be having. You're losing out gaining quality knowledge from people that can empower you. Of course motivation and inspiration come from within, but we can never underestimate the influence of positive relationships with like-minded friends and associates.

Putting off challenges: Are you a procrastinator? Are you doing things that don't really matter to avoid doing the things that do matter? Every time we don't act, we push it back.

Over Thinking: Are you a perfectionist? There is no perfect moment to start some new idea. When you over think something, you over analysis to the point where you come up with a reason why it can't be done. Nothing can be achieved in life until you actually get started, take action and put it out there.

You can't improve on something that you haven't yet started.

Exercise 2: Releasing what is stopping you from being successful.

Step 1: Write down a list of things that are stopping you from being successful. Once again be honest with yourself. It could be from the examples above or you could have your own patterns that you have developed which are blocking your success. It could be a limiting belief you have, that you have carried around with you. It could be something simple.

Take time to think about this and start off this exercise by asking yourself these two questions:

What do I really want to achieve in my life?

What is stopping me from having that success right now?

List as many things as you think are appropriate.

Get them out of your head, onto paper, so that you can let them go.

Step 2: Once you have your list of all the things you believe are stopping you from moving forward; take your list and find a match or lighter. Then burn the list. As you watch the paper and all the obstacles that have been holding you back burn with it, give yourself that feeling of release. Know you are letting go of these limitations and have made the decision to start afresh.

"If you always do what you've always done, you'll always get what you've always got."

(Henry Ford)

It's time to do something different.

3

How Do You Take Responsibility for Your Life? Decide to!

"It is in your moments of decisions that your destiny is shaped"

(Tony Robbins)

The Power of Choice

When we are faced with any situation in life we always have more than one choice as to how to proceed. Whatever decision we make in that moment will determine what comes next in our life. At any time, you can also choose to stop doing something that is not working in your life and you can decide to do something different, that will lead you in another direction.

I'm sure everyone reading this book can think back to a decision you made years ago, that if you had of made a different decision then would have taken you on a different path in life. Today is no different! Today, as you read through the pages of this book, could be a major breakthrough in your life because you have made a decision to take responsibility for your life in a certain area. You also made the decision to no longer blame other people, circumstances or your past for where you are in your life right now. For success to happen in your life you need to get into the habit of opening your mind up to new choices because no matter where you are right now, you already have 2 choices:

- You can choose to stay where you are or
- You can choose to change.

Adam's Story

Adam came to me totally distraught and ready to give up on life. He was a carpenter and worked on building sites, helping with the development of new housing estates. One day, for no apparent reason at all, he broke down and started to weep uncontrollably. He started shaking and within a few minutes was experiencing huge levels of anxiety. His work colleagues called paramedics and he was reluctantly taken to the nearest hospital. For six months after that he became lost in his own thoughts and was diagnosed with depression. When he was told what was wrong with him, he became worse and found it hard to function on a daily basis. He didn't sleep at nights and because he had little or no sleep some nights, he didn't feel like doing anything during the day and stopped eating. So life was, in his words, a total waste of time. Before he came to my office I was told by a family member that he had been to see a psychologist and was currently seeing a counsellor on a daily basis. When he walked into my therapy room he looked at my chair and I could see by the look on his face he was thinking, "oh here we go again, more talking."

I got him a glass of cold water, asked him to wait for a moment and I went and got my coat.

We have a beautiful nature walk beside my office that incorporates a small river and some beautiful moments of nature so I came back into the room and took him there. We walked for around an hour and I started talking to him about what he liked to do before he became, "sick". He talked about sport, coaching football, going to the gym, running every day, going down to his county house in South of Ireland and within five or ten minutes he was perky. I talked to him about taking responsibility for his life and about choice and helped him focus on two simple things that could help him make a small change in how he felt right now. By the time we got back to my office he had two new choices he didn't think he had before, because he had been so focused on what he was going through and how he was letting everyone down. I explained how he was using his imagination to work against him. I also explained how he could retrain his imagination to work for him, making him feel better within himself. The "baggage he was carrying on his shoulders, that was weighing him down" as he put it, was left in the river at the nature walk. We decided he didn't need it anymore because it was just a product of his imagination. After a few sessions his sleeping had improved and he was getting back into life again. I told him on that first session that he had two choices; he could accept this thing called depression or he could choose to change and accept life, taking small steps to move in the direction that would make him feel better. As he was so down on himself, at that moment and didn't really care too much for himself I reframed that he could do it for his wife and four beautiful children and be the rock he always was for them. He made this change and decided to take back control of his life again. His journey to get back on track was not a quick fix and was going to take him some time. By making the initial decision that his life was worth more than he was giving, was the first step. He could now commit to spending each day doing something that would improve his mind set, putting new information into his mind each day to improve the quality of his life.

You are a product of all the choices you have made in the past and if you don't like where you are then you can certainly change it. The circumstances of your life simply reveal what kind of choices you have made up until this present moment. You don't have to stay the same; it's your choice. Sometimes in life things just don't work out. When these things happen we can choose to look for reasons and go into an endless loop or we can choose to learn from these experiences and start a new process of thinking how to have a more productive, happier experience in the future.

From this moment forward you are faced with a choice to put the principles in this book into practice or to go back and live the life you have been living before. Now if you are living a life that is exciting and fulfilling then you have an amazing gift but if you want to change, then it's your choice and you do that simply by deciding to. It's not complicated. At this stage don't get caught up in "how" this will happen, that comes later. Remember changing your life is one small step at a time and making that initial decision is all you need to focus on right now. But when you make that decision you also decide to no longer get caught up in what is missing in your life; what is wrong with you and what should have happened up to now. You put your attention and your intentions on what it is you want to shift and change.

"What is necessary to change a person, is to change his awareness of himself."

(A.Maslow)

Making that decision to take full responsibility for your life means you choose how to life your life. Success is not an accident. It is a very structured way of thinking, behaving and doing. You become successful in life one day at a time, by using a simple set of principles and rituals that have been proven time and time again. Principles that I will take you through in the following chapters of this book.

So let's not labour over this point any longer. Make your choice and then decide to follow through, as we move onto, in my opinion, one of the most important key factors of lasting success and achievement.

The Power of Belief in Yourself

When you hear people talking about success, they talk about determination, persistence, hard work, focus etc. These are all key factors in the journey to success and will be covered as we go through this book. But in your journey to succeed there is something so much more powerful that you need to develop, which will carry you through. That is belief in yourself. Belief in yourself is the critical element for your success in life.

When you go through the first stages of your life you buy into a number of beliefs, by very meaningful people, attempting to convince you that you have certain limitation in life:

"You can't do this."

"This isn't possible."

"You don't have the ability."

"Better sticking with what you know."

"Don't get caught up in all that stuff, you don't want to get hurt, when it all goes wrong."

When you start buying into those beliefs, you start developing that mentality of limitation. You develop the belief that who you are is all you are capable of being. You develop that "herd like" mentality and you simply fit in to other people's way of thinking.

People will die for certain beliefs, countries are at war for their beliefs and the majority of people are imprisoned in their mind by their limiting beliefs.

But what is a belief and how can we change the ones that don't serve us and develop new ones?

A belief is simply a thought that has been reinforced

through repetition over and over, that is now acted upon as if reality.

A belief is simply a way of thinking. If you have the belief that "I'm not smart" or "I'm too old" or "I could never achieve that."

What has happened, is that at one time, you had to create a thought in your mind, for the first time, of this limitation and then as you developed those thoughts over and over you adopted that thinking as true. But as already stated in the beginning of this chapter, we are choice making individuals and our thinking can change; we can decide to no longer adopt that limiting belief and start to believe something else that serves us better and will empower us to success.

As human beings we are creatures of habit and beliefs are simply habitual ways of thinking we act upon, that run automatically. But habits can be changed by finding out the opposite of what you have been doing and starting to practice that on a daily basis until you develop a new habit. The start of that is going back to your thoughts and working from there. A habit is an idea or series of thoughts that have been fixed in our sub-conscious minds and run automatically. Through making new conscious choices, we can renew the mind and form new habits and new beliefs.

Beliefs are made up, so my theory is that if you're going to make something up, why now start to make up something that will empower you rather than limit you. You need to have a belief that will support you in your quest for your new goal or success because it is the belief that will guide you toward your outcome. If you set yourself a goal and want to change a certain area of your life, but you don't believe you will achieve it, or you believe you are not worthy of it, then those unconscious beliefs will stop you from achieving that goal, no matter how much willpower you attempt to use.

Napoleon Hill, in his great book, "Think and grow rich" said:

"What the mind can conceive and believe: The mind can achieve, regardless of how many times he has tried and failed".

I believe this statement to be 100% accurate but there is a part of that statement that is missing in people's lives. It is the missing ingredient that is preventing people from greatness in life.

We all have an imagination so we can all conceive in our minds what we would really like to achieve in life. However, what I have found over the past 10 years, in working with clients from all walks of life, is that there is a huge majority of people who actually don't believe in themselves and their ability to get what they want. That lack of belief is one of the key components that is keeping them back.

So how do you change a belief?

If you are carrying around a set of beliefs that are in opposition with what you want, you have created them at some point in your life. By releasing these old beliefs, you can start a mental process of building new beliefs that will empower you.

Find out what limiting beliefs you have in your life and start challenging them. I use a simple formula with my clients that I will share with you to help identify limiting beliefs and how to adopt new ones. But let me show you one of the best ways to change anything if your life through a process of questions.

Questions, are the answer to your success

If you have been consciously following this book you will notice that up to now I have been asking you question after question. The title of each chapter is a question and I have continued to ask them repeatedly throughout, for the simple reason I believe that questions are the key to making new decisions. The questions you habitually ask yourself will elicit a response, whether it be negative or positive, whether it be empowering or disempowering. Just like every skill you acquire in life there is a process to follow in asking the right questions. That skill, like any other skill in life, needs to be practiced through repetition to run automatically.

What kind of questions do you habitually ask yourself when faced with a situation?

When it comes to internal questions most people, unconsciously, are asking themselves, what I call, endless loop questions; that keep them contained in that very problem they are trying to overcome.

When you ask yourself a question, the brain has to search for the answer. Most of the time it will go into your database and give you the answers you have been telling yourself over and over again.

Have a read through the following questions below:

- Why can't I do this vs How can I turn this around and make it work?
- Why is this happening to me? vs What can I do to change this?
- How could they do this to me? vs How can I learn from this experience to help me move on?
- Why can't I ever make money? vs How can I add more value to what I am doing right now to increase my income?
- What's wrong in my life? vs What am I grateful for in my life right now?
- Why do I always fail vs What could I be doing differently in these situations, that I haven't done before, that could get me better results than I am getting right now?

If you look at the above questions, I'm sure you will agree that the two questions given on each line will elicit a totally different response. People usually get caught up in "Why" questions that mostly bring about the wrong answer and can actually make you feel even worse than when they asked themselves the question in the first place, e.g.

"Why does this always happen to me?"

"Why do I never succeed?"

"Why am I such a failure?"

"Why do I even bother?"

"Why is my life such a mess?"

If you read back through these questions; how positive do you feel and what kind of answers do you get?

So let's try a better set of questions that you can ask yourself when faced with a challenge in life?

As you go through this next exercise, think of an issue you have had recently and go ask yourself the following questions to see how you can come up with a solution.

Exercise 3: Empowering Questions

What does this mean to me?

What else could it mean if I choose a different meaning that could empower me in this situation?

How could I adapt that new meaning and make it part of my thinking?

If I was to adopt this meaning into my life, what could be different than before?

How could I move forward in a positive way?

What one small step could I take right now to change this situation?

What's great about this situation that I never thought about before?

What can I learn from this situation?

What could I be doing each day to make this new way of thinking become a habit?

How could I start that process right now?

When there is no enemy within, the enemy outside can do us no harm.

(African Proverb)

4

Fear: It's All in Your Head

"Remember this, with every experience in which you look fear in the face,
you gain inner strength and confidence.

So spread your wings, open doors and go for it.

The opportunity is all yours"

(Lisa Desatnik)

In this chapter I want to touch on the concept of fear and how to move past it. As this is a book about mastering yourself and achievement, I want to focus on fear in the context of stopping you from stretching yourself, and going out and achieving something in your life. Most people don't shoot for their goals and dreams because of some internal fear that is controlling them.

When you look at life, the only time we have is "now." Yesterday has already happened, so it's gone, and tomorrow has not arrived yet, so right now at this moment, it doesn't exist.

When people have fear, it is simply because they are not living life, they are simply living in their mind. Fear is always about what is going to happen next. You can't be afraid of the past because the past has already come and gone, so the fear is always about the future. So if you think about it, you are always afraid of something that doesn't yet exist. Fear is a simple over excessive use of your imagination that creates a physical feeling inside of you, which reaches various levels of strength and stops you from progressing in a certain area in your life. The more you use your imagination to reinforce that fear, then the stronger the physical symptoms become, to the point where it can be so over whelming that you don't even try. The fear becomes a controlling factor and overrides any rational attempt you make. But if you think about it, if your fear is about the future, which doesn't exist, then your fear is entirely imaginary. The imagination is such a powerful thing and overrides willpower every time.

"When the will and the imagination are in conflict, the imagination will win out every time."

People are always suffering in one way or another; either what happened yesterday or what may happen tomorrow. So your suffering is always about that which does not exist, simply because you're not rooted in the "now," which is the only reality. Instead you're lost in your imagination, that's the basis of your fear. If you were rooted in reality, there would be no fear. To live life with little or no fear you simply make the decision to start living in the moment, in the now. And when you start practicing living in the moment, your enjoyment, happiness and fulfilment in life becomes tenfold.

Fear is not a product of life. Fear is a product of your imagination and your thoughts. You are suffering inside that which does not exist because you are rooted, not in reality, but in your mind which is constantly focusing on the past and associating that with the future. You don't actually know anything about the future. In your mind you take a piece of the past, apply make-up on it in the form of thoughts and images and think of it as your future. You then act on that or not act on that as if it's real.

"You can plan your future today but you cannot live in your future today."

But right now people, in their minds, are living in tomorrow today and that is why there is fear. The only thing you can do about this is, come down to reality and start living in the moment. If you just respond to what is there right now and not imagine something that does not exist, with practice you can start to eliminate the fear.

Think about it this way; once you retrain your mind to live in the "now," and actually start experiencing and living in the now what happens to the fear. It goes away because you are not allowing yourself to use your imagination to imagine something that does not exist. Therefore, you will only respond to what exists right now.

I'm sure as you read this chapter you will all have experienced some kind of fear to a certain situation in your life;

Fear of failure,

Fear of public speaking,

Fear of starting a business,

Fear of interviews,

Fear of success,

Fear of the future etc.

Maybe that fear has controlled you for a period of time and stopped you from living the life you really want to live. Maybe for some of you this is still the case.

This book is about change and standing up for yourself. Finding new ways to retrain your sub-conscious mind to process things differently, and help you overcome fear.

Taking responsibility for your life means deciding whether you are going to start experiencing the life you want to life, on your terms, and also choosing no longer to avoid life.

When you combine inner strength with a burning desire to succeed, then fear can no longer overwhelm you.

Just as an athlete can build up strength over a period of time to become superior at what he does, you can also develop that inner strength and intensity in the achievement of your goal. The moment you use fear as a tool to protect yourself, your intensity goes down. Once it goes down, your ability to experience life to the full starts to diminish. But either way you have a choice; it's all in your mind. You make it up as you go along, through your imagination.

So once again, as I have already said, my theory is that if you're going to make stuff up, then start using your imagination to make up good stuff, that empowers you and gives you the strength and intensity to crush that old fear. You will never experience anything amazing when you are fearful, but when you learn to move beyond that fear, better things happen in your life.

How can you overcome something that doesn't really exist?

As I was developing my practice as a clinical hypnotherapist, I would deal with lots of people that had a wide variety of fears. There are all sorts of crazy names for them, labels society has put on these fears. But as time progressed and I learned my craft, I adopted the very belief I am sharing with you now, that fear is simply a product if our imagination. The only thing we really fear is something in the future that doesn't even exist.

So when you think about it, how can you overcome something that doesn't even exist? You can't! But once you start to see it as I'm explaining it to you, you soon realize you don't have to. Once you start to reframe it, the fear is replaced and you take back control.

The results we get in life are based on how we approach each situation we are faced with. When a situation arises that brings with it fear, if you allow your imagination to play tricks and overwhelm you, then the fear will dictate what results you get.

So rather than trying to overcome fear, I simply teach people to focus on what they want instead.

Many clients would come into my office and say things like,

"I don't want to be overweight,"

"I don't want to smoke anymore, I'm sick of it,"

"I don't want to have this fear," I don't like being this way, it's ruining my life."

The problem with all of these is that when you are trying to "stop doing" something in your mind or overcome something, it simply does not work. You are constantly reinforcing the very thing you want to overcome. Let me give you an example:

Exercise:

For the next 20 seconds I **don't** want you to think of the colour blue: So your job is **not** to think of the colour blue. So whatever you do, **don't think** of the colour blue. Remember I **don't want you to think** of the colour blue....

So what happened? As I was telling you not to think of the colour blue, that was the only thing that was going through your mind. Blue was the only thing you were thinking of because I told you not to. You were thinking of blue, right.

Now take someone who is trying to overcome a fear of public speaking; they are constantly telling themselves, "I don't want to make a fool of myself, I just can't stand up there feeling this way." They are constantly impressing upon the subconscious the very thing they don't want, so what they are really doing, is reinforcing it.

So how then do we get rid of fear?

Let's go back to the "blue "example and use it as a metaphor to explain the alternative.

If someone came to me and they didn't want to think of blue anymore (blue being the weight, smoking, public speaking, the future etc.) then what I would do is to get them to focus on green (what they want instead: to be healthier and slimmer, to become a non-smoker, to become a confident public speaker etc.) We would talk about green; getting them to use their imagination to reinforce it, linking confidence and excitement with it. I would have them focus solely on want they wanted instead, feeling so much pleasure to the new behaviour. I get them to go through "the green" for a few days and really use their imagination to not only see the green, but feel it, experience it, getting their mind to rehearse it over and over again.

Now as we have been talking about the green and reinforcing it; what have we not mentioned or even talked about anymore? The blue.

By shifting our focus and using the imagination to reinforce something totally different and linking massive pleasure to this new idea, it becomes our reality. You are breaking the old neuro-association and replacing it with a new pattern that is different and one that feels much better. Then by repetition you are anchoring and conditioning it in your nervous system so that it runs automatically. This takes a bit of practice (as everything else does in life) but if you really want to overcome something, you will always find a way, using whatever is necessary, taking whatever time it takes.

Whatever you focus on in life, you manifest, and when you are constantly focusing on the fear, which as we discussed earlier is based on something that doesn't even exist yet, you are simply using your imagination to create this illusion, you act out on it, it becomes your reality and through practice this become habit.

The alternative is to start the process of retraining your mind and using your imagination to work with you instead of against you. It's your mind remember; it is there to do whatever you want it to do. If you allow fear to control you regularly then it becomes habit. You have created a habit that is no longer serving you. Just like the habit of over eating or smoking, when you get to the stage where enough is enough, when you are sick and tired of being sick and tired of over eating or smoking, then you can decide to stop practicing it and retrain your mind to build up a new habit as a non-smoker or healthier, slimmer person. Well if you can do that in one aspect of your life, then you can do it with all aspects. And if you can train your imagination to create fear, "the blue," then you can go through the same process to create the alternative, which is the very thing you want to achieve, "the green."

Movies in your mind.

I'm sure you have sat down and enjoyed a good horror movie at some stage in your life. You were probably afraid at certain points of the movie, but at some level you knew if wasn't real. It was just a bunch of actors on a screen, some music and a plot. But it didn't stop you from being afraid, because your imagination took over. When the movie finished you were fine and you went about your day as normal. Movie producers and actors make a lot of money out of films because then ignite your imagination.

Don't we do the same thing with our minds? We create a movie inside our mind of what could happen to us in the future. We run this movie in our minds over and over again and each time we do it our imagination reinforces the fear, compounds the fear and this becomes habit and maybe even a belief. It's nothing more than a bad habit and a limiting belief. The big difference is that when you are running your movie in your mind of what you fear, you're not making any money out of it, and it's affecting your life in a negative way. It's simply your imagination and by letting it continue you are allowing your mind to stop you from actually experiencing what you really want instead.

So if you have the power to change it, why the hell go through it any longer, if you could spend your time doing something else which is even better.

Fear means that you are producing horror movies in your mind that only you are willing to watch, but it is you that is producing them each time through your imagination.

In his book, "Super coach," Michael Neill says:

"You are never afraid of what you think you are afraid of; You are only afraid of what you think."

It's not spiders or heights or the future that scare us, it's simply our internal pictures and thoughts of the spiders and heights that scare us. When we teach ourselves to deal with the cause, our thoughts and our imagination, not the future, then the fear will diminish and dissipate.

I once had a client who came to me with fear of spiders. She was so scared of spiders, of any size, that she couldn't even look at a picture of one without panicking. I told her that I had a spider in a locked box downstairs and I would show it to her at the end of the session. At this she automatically freaked out, taking me around five minutes to calm her down. I explained to her how she created the fear through her imagination, and by giving her a few examples she could related them to her fear of spiders. This helped her understand what was going on in her mind. We were able to establish how she was making literally making it up. Her fear was simply generated by her thoughts of the spider in the future, not the actual spider itself. There was no spider. She had created a movie in her mind using her imagination and the movie created the fear.

Remember you are the producer of your own internal movies. If you don't like the ones you're producing right now, produce something else. Produce a comedy, a love story, an action movie, a movie that makes you happy and excited.

Actually do it now as you're reading this. See what it is you were afraid of and using your imagination, simply close your eyes and see yourself doing that what your feared easily and effortlessly, gaining new insights, and as you go through this think about how this makes your feel. Remember it's your imagination, you can do whatever you want.

I will go through an in-depth exercise at the end of this chapter to help you with this.

The point I am trying to make, is that the fear you are experiencing is a way you have been using your mind in a certain way, it has become a pattern. From this moment forward, start using your mind differently and you will create a different result, developing a different pattern.

I want to finish off this chapter by addressing the fear of failure, a huge factor in many people's lives.

Karen's Story

Karen was a nurse in a local hospital. She had been in nursing for almost 15 years and was the head of her ward. She was excellent at her job and had so much job satisfaction that she was liked and admired by almost everyone she came across, both her work colleagues and her patients. She had this ambition to go for a senior post in the hospital which meant taking a step up from nursing and becoming a ward manager, dealing with the day to day running of a section of the hospital. She was totally competent and confident in her ability to do this and this was a position that she wanted very much. The job opportunity came up for her the year before she came to see me and she applied for the interview. She went for the interview and when she walked into the room she totally froze. She forgot everything she knew and, in her words, came out of the interview looking like someone who hadn't a clue what she was talking about. The promotion passed her by.

Six months later another position came up and she once again applied for the job. This time as the interview approached she began to panic. Two weeks before the interview, she starting thinking of her previous experience and what a disaster it had been and how this next interview would probably be even worse. She sees herself in her imagination sitting in the interview (which hadn't even happened yet), a nervous wreck and once again leaving the room looking silly, but this time it was ten times worse. She used her imagination to create the worst possible scenario. With one week to go she could feel herself going into panic mode and feeling anxious every time she thought about being in the room in front of the board. On the day of the interview, as she drove to work, she became so afraid of failing and messing up again, that she didn't even go into the interview. Instead she drove around and cried uncontrollably for a couple of hours. Needless to say, another chance had passed her by. She had to take a couple of days leave from work to help her deal with the feeling of loss and disappointment. She returned to work and went about her daily routine as best she could and tried to put the whole situation out of her head.

When she came to me, she was faced with another interview, except this time it was an emergency interview and for that reason there was only one person holding the interview instead of four. I started our session by having her focus on how her life would change if she got the position and what it would mean to her. We focused on "the green." She talked about this being her, "dream job." I had her anchor all these positive feelings and reinforced them with a few great memories she had from her past. I taught her a few techniques that would help her focus on what was important in the interview, instead of what didn't matter (the blue), and I got her to listen to a hypnotic audio each night before she went to bed to help her relax and unwind. She went for the interview, got the job and is now doing what she loves. She was able to make the decision that her fear was not real and simply a product of her imagination. She was then able to use her imagination to break the old pattern and focus on what she wanted instead.

You're going to fail in life. There is no getting away from it and there is no need to be afraid.

Fear of failure can eat people up inside. The very thought of failing is enough to totally immobilise people to the point where they quit altogether.

But what is fear of failure and why must you "accept failure" rather than fear it?

Having a fear of failure is always about "what if." Once again it is about using your imagination, going into a future in your mind that doesn't yet exist and running your movie of possibilities of things going wrong.

"What if I fail in this new business venture?"

"What if I get it wrong?"

"What if I mess up?"

"What if this doesn't work out for me?"

"What if I don't get it right?"

The truth is when you attempt something for the first time and start something new, you're going to fail more often than you succeed. You're going to get it wrong many times, you're going to mess up and you're not always going to get it right, especially not the first time.

Remember when you got into a car for the first time when you started to learn how to drive. You didn't get it right the first time. You messed up many times and got it wrong, but did you give up? No! You learned, through repetition, to succeed. You made mistakes along the way, failing almost every single driving lesson at something, but you learned from your failures and persisted until it worked out.

Succeeding at anything is life in no different. We just make the task most stressful in our minds. The only time we have is now. If you learn to focus on the now and learn from your mistakes, then you can become more successful, because you're not worried about your future. Once you have dealt with each day you have had an experience so you move onto the next. With each day comes a new experience and with each experience you build your confidence along the way. Remember what you continuously focus on in your life, you manifest.

So if I had to write a formula for overcoming fear of failure in a few simple steps, it would go something like this:

Step1: Try something new, maybe fail and get it wrong.

Step 2: Find out what it is you did that made it wrong.

Step 3: Learn a better way, try again.

Step 4: Maybe mess up again and fail a few more times.

Step 5: Learn from your mistakes. Try again with a better understanding.

Step 6: Get it better this time. Learn from what you have done and also gain a bit of confidence along the way.

Step 7: Try again. Get it right this time.

Step 8: Try it a few more times to become competent at what you have learned so that this becomes a habit. Gain more confidence along the way.

Step 9: Acknowledge that step as being a success. Enjoy the process and give yourself a pat on the back for that small success.

Step 10: Move on to the next step and repeat the process from step 1.

But wait, what about the fear of failure in the steps?

Sorry but if you were just to follow these simple steps, you would be so involved in what you were doing (the green), you wouldn't have time to think about any fear because there would be any. When you work in the "now," there is no fear. You get used to the failures because you now accept that they are a big part of the process; you have a different perspective of failure, you no longer fear it, you embrace it. It becomes an adrenaline rush instead of a feeling of paralysis. Am I saying you are never going to be fearful about anything in life? No, not at all, but once you feel that fear coming on, you realise where it is coming from and you start eliminating it by retraining your nervous system to develop the green in the situation.

When I worked for a direct sales company in my early 30's, we had to do a lot of cold calling on householder's door to door. If we managed to get into a house, we had to put on a presentation and try to sell the occupier a very expensive product that they had no intention of buying. I hated this experience. Don't get me wrong, I loved the job as there were different opportunities of advancement in the company. I loved the challenge of doing something different each day but I hated the first initial step, selling door to door, but it had to be done.

I failed miserable day after day, because I let the fear consume me.

Each day I was so afraid of failing that, by the time I got to a house, I hadn't a chance of selling anything. At the start I made a few sales, out of pity, but I had the worst sales conversion rate in the company. I was so up in my head about what could happen, that by the time I got to each client, even though I really wanted them to buy; my body language, my attitude; my Mind-Set was all screaming out, "You wouldn't want to buy one of these." That was the results I got time after time. I think I developed a phobia of selling because I could feel myself shaking and my mouth drying up. I dropped everything, so I looked clumsy and I always needed to use the bathroom when I went into a house due to panic. Not a great platform to pitch a fifteen-hundred-pound product to a potential client. To be honest at the start of my sales career I didn't even see the people as potential clients, I was just hoping someone would feel sorry for me and buy something. But

I was a hard worker and I could see the potential in the job as other sales reps stood up every day and told of their successes and they showed me their commission checks every week, so I knew it wasn't all bullshit.

I remember one Friday afternoon, after a horrible week, I was ready to quit as I felt I was getting nowhere. The director of the company persuaded me to spend the next few days with an experienced sales rep who was good at closing sales and getting into see clients. He told me that if I wanted to quit after that then that was fine and he even offered me a financial bonus just for sitting watching this guy for a couple of days. What did I have to lose? I spent a few days with him and this experience totally changed the way I did things from that moment forward.

On the first day with this experienced sales rep, as we drove to our first presentation, I was thinking of all the things I was doing wrong, how this guy would be the best at what he did. I couldn't wait to see a master at his work. By watching his presentation on the first day, I was totally shocked. I was able to make the assumption within the first couple of presentations that my presentation was much better than his. There was one thing I noticed, right from I got into his car that was totally different in what he did; failure was not an option. He had no fear of knocking on ten doors only to be told to bugger off, sometimes doors being slammed in his face, because of his aggressive style. He had no fear of asking for the order over and over after the client had already said no. There was no room for failing in what he did.

As I chatted to him in between presentations, I told him of my fear of failing and how it consumed me. What he told me then really changed my attitude towards my sales presentation, to the point I moved up in the company to his level within the next few months.

He told me that when he started his week he set himself a goal of failing ten times that week. If he failed ten times, then he achieved his goal and he gave himself a treat. I thought this was absurd. As he went on to explain this further he explained that he would go into each house and give the best presentation he could give. He knew he had a one in three conversation rate, so each day he must fail at least twice before he made his sale. He made failure part of his routine and embraced it to the point that it was just the norm. It became such a routine that when he failed to sell a product in a house, he turned it around in his mind by shaking the hand of the householder on the way out saying, "I want to thank you for not buying from me, I have a one in three conversation rate and you are the second person that hasn't bought from me so my next client will buy, thank you again so much and have an amazing day." When I heard him say this the first couple of times, I found this the funniest thing I had ever heard. Not at what he said, but the reaction of the person whose hand he was shaking. As they shook his hand the reaction on their face was priceless, thinking, "here is this crazy salesman who has tortured me to buy his product for the last two hours, having told him no a hundred times and he is thanking me for not buying." But it worked for him! He left the house feeling up beat, motivated and "on fire" and straight onto the house next door. The people in the next house had no chance of not buying from him and they didn't even know they were about to buy something.

His goal for each week was to experience ten failures and he didn't stop until ten people had said no. Yet, by the time he had achieved the ten failures, he achieved his sales target as well. He made failure a part of what he did and his conversion rate became better, his confidence grew and he had totally eliminated fear from his profession.

If you look at any successful person in any field, the reason they are so successful is because they have probably failed the more times and that why they are successful

Basketball legend Michael Jordan sums it up like this:

"I've missed more than 9000 shots in my career. I've lost almost 300 games. 26 times, I've been trusted to take the game winning shot and missed. I've failed over and over and over again in my life. And that is why I succeed."

(Michael Jordan)

Exercise 4: Spinning Your Fears

If you cannot get your head around the concept that fear is not real, then try this approach. The next exercise I want to share with you is a simple exercise I use with some clients to help them move beyond their fears.

1) *Think of the thing or situation that generated the fear in you.*

2) *As you think about it where does that feeling start in your body (I'm not too worried about the things you're afraid of but focus on the feeling). If you can't get scared right now, force yourself to think of the thing that scares you and see if you can bring up some of that feeling associated to that thing or event and notice where the feeling is on your body.*

3) *Now as you continue to think about it, notice where the fear travels to (if the feeling stayed in one place it would dissipate and fade but for fear to generate it has to travel through your body). Does it go up or down? If it starts in your stomach or your chest where does it travel to in your body next? And in what direction does in travel, up or down, e.g. stomach to chest to neck or stomach to legs to feet etc....*

4) *Notice does it spin toward you or away from you? If it doesn't feel as though it's spinning, ask yourself which way it would be spinning if it were. This could be toward you or away from, spinning from front to back or from side to side).*

5) *I want you to use your imagination and imagine that you're pulling the spinning fear out of your body so you can see it in front of you. You can see it spinning towards you and it's all happening in front of your body right now.*

6) *Now I want you to turn it upside down so now it's spinning the opposite way of what it was originally.*

7) *Think of your favourite colour and give it that colour.*

8) *So if you're favourite colour is blue, make it that colour and imagine it's spinning away from you and I want you to put it right back inside your body. Bring it back inside your*

body so you can feel it spinning down through your chest and up your back, up to the top of your head and back down your chest. It's spinning away from you and it's a bright blue colour. Notice how that feels.

9) Now spin it faster and notice that as you spin it faster you get a different feeling and as you spin it even faster that good feeling becomes stronger.

I want you to take that great feeling and let it spread from the top of your head down to the tips of your toes, right out to the edges of your fingertips. The more you spin the feeling, the easier it will be for you to have this feeling anytime you want just by taking control of it - because it's not just a feeling, it's your feeling and if you use your imagination enough you can create that good feeling anytime you want, replacing the old feeling, that you don't need any more.

How Do You Think

If you think you are beaten, you are;
If you think you dare not, you don't!
If you'd like to win, but you think you can't,
It's almost certain you won't.

If you think you'll lose, you're lost;
For out in the world we find
Success begins with a fellow's will;
It's all in the state of mind!

If you think you're outclassed, you are;
You've got to think high to rise.
You've got to be sure of yourself
Before you'll ever win the prize.

Life's battles don't always go
To the stronger or faster man;
But sooner or later the man who wins
Is the person who thinks he can!

(Anonymous)

Part 2

Renewing Your Mind for
Success

"Progress is impossible without change, and those who cannot change their minds cannot change anything."

(George Bernard Shaw)

5

Ten Steps for Change!

"You must develop the right psychology to succeed in life and that starts with renewing your mind.

Putting new ideas into your mind and through repetition reinforcing those ideas emotionally until they become habit; until it runs automatically and becomes part of who you are."

(Robert Herdman)

I want to start off this section by giving you my ten steps for change formula that I use with all my clients as part of the first steps in my coaching program. These steps are a recap of some of the things we have already discussed and a few of the things we will go onto discuss in the next few chapters.

These were one of the first set of learning's I reinforced into my mind each day as I started my career. Although they are very basic concepts, it's the process of going back to basics and retraining your mind that develops a new Mind-Set.

So here are my basic 10 Steps to Change:

1) **Decide to:** As we have already discussed in chapter three, you must make that ultimate decision. This decision is not knowing you ought to change, it is a decision you are making that there is no going back. This has got to be first and foremost if true lasting change is going to happen in your life. A true decision is totally different from "trying." When people say to me, I'll "try" it's like they are telling themselves an honest lie. There is no try at this stage, it's either "do or don't do" and if you are not willing to make that ultimate decision, then the rest of this book is no use to you, it's simply a novel to pass time. What's the point? Nothing will become a reality in your life without that initial decision.

"A true decision is the open door to reality."

You and you alone are the only one that can open the door for the process of change. Remember being sick and tired of your life and wanting to change is not enough to change it. It has to be more than that.

In my profession I meet a lot of people who don't like the way their lives have turned out and they all have their own story of why. I'm sure you have yours as well. Your story is not going to change your life. You have to make the decision that you are no longer willing to accept this any longer and decide to give it your all. Enough said on this point.

2) **Desire:** Not only do you have to make a decision to change but you have to have a strong desire to change. You can never change based on someone else's desires. If you really want to lose weight and you desire for chocolate is stronger than your desire for being healthier and slimmer, you will always go for the chocolate. A desire is something that drives you inside. When you have that desire for success and you take continuous action, that desire becomes a passion.

3) **Your Reasons:** You must know "WHY" you are doing what you're doing. The stronger your why's are and the more you have, the more you will be driven to achieve your goal. You have to have reasons why you are doing what you are doing. If you ask any successful person, they always know what it is they want and the reasons why they are doing it. You have to have purpose because that purpose will drive you, especially when times are hard. Purpose provides drive. When you have enough reasons; you build a big enough why and you can figure out how to do about anything. It's your driving force. In an earlier chapter I asked you to write down a list of why's in your journal. Open that page and once again go through your Why's.

4) **Renew your knowledge base:** People are being held back in life for what they don't know. Your knowledge base must increase if your life experiences are going to increase. You can have the best will in the world and a burning desire to become a boxing champion, but if you step into the ring and haven't got the knowledge base and the skill, then you're going to get hurt. You may

want to start your own business and become an entrepreneur but if you don't have enough information on how to run a business you're going to fail. You need to have the right Mind-Set in good times and in challenging times for continued success. You have to become a constant leaner and update your knowledge base to develop the skills in whatever it is you're trying to achieve, to become a success. If your knowledge base is shallow and small, then your experience will be shallow and small. As you increase your knowledge base, along the way to your success, you increase the quality of your experiences along the way.

When you build up a knowledge base of how the mind works then you begin to understand how you get yourself into the situations you do and therefore are able to see those patterns and develop new ones. If you go about on a daily basis being governed by your emotions, the danger is your emotions change more than you do. One day you're going to feel like doing something and the next day you're not going to feel the same way. When you recognise the patterns, you can change them.

5) **Diligence:** Applying the things you know day in, day out is a major part of the change process. It is not what you do one time that is going to be responsible for your success in life. It is what you are willing to do on a consistent basis that matters. Being successful is getting up every day, living by a set of rituals (which we will cover in a later chapter) and putting these ritual into place today

and tomorrow and the next day and the next; despite the challenges, despite the opinions of other people and whether you feel like it or not. This is how you build new habits and becoming successful is all about habit.

When I chat to people who are successful, no matter what field it is, there is always one commonality. They all have a set of ritual that they put into place and they get up each morning and go through these rituals until the day ends. They get up the next morning and repeat the process because it's what they do, it's who they have become, and there is no other way. It's now a habit and I call that the "Success Habit."

This is not rocket science but sadly it is what is missing in people's lives and this lack of diligence eventually results in failure, giving up and making excuses.

When you start a pattern of diligence then you start to create a new habit. Consistently thinking new thought and making better decisions starts the process of change.

But it's not going to happen because of what you did one day or one week; change doesn't happen in a day but it does happen daily.

6) **Defend your mind against old thoughts:** What goes into your mind on a daily basis becomes who you are. Developing yourself mentally is just as important as achieving the goal. Being in a new career with an old Mind-Set will just not work because sooner or later those weeds will come up and begin to surface again. It's important to

change your thoughts by conditioning your mind daily with new material that will help you develop an "unstoppable Mind-Set." This means listening to new speakers, reading new books, listening to audios of people who are successful in your chosen path, watching videos of successful people, getting as much new information as possible that will override the old thought pattern you developed in the past.

The life you are living right now is the result of how you have set your mind in the past. If you want to have consistent change you need to update your software so that your future is better than what you are producing right now.

No matter what you are trying to achieve in life; a better relationship, building a new business, learning a new skill, becoming financially independent, or whatever success means to you. It is so important to develop the Mind-Set of that person you want to become along the way, defending your mind against old programming by renewing your mind. This is how change lasts and success continues. If your Mind-Set stays the same, then your life stays the same.

If your Mind-Set stays the same, then your marriage stays the same.

If your Mind-Set stays the same, then your business stays the same. The truth is that nothing in life ever stays the same, we are either growing or we are dying. Working on your Mind-Set on a daily basis and defending your mind against old thoughts is probably one of the most important gifts you can give yourself.

7) **Dissociate yourself from the past:** We have covered this in an earlier chapter but I want to briefly summarise it again because it is such an important step.

You may feel comfortable with some of your old ties, some of your old relationships, some of your old habits etc. but it can be these very things that can be holding your back and stopping you from getting to the place you want to be in your life.

There are certain people that you must dissociate from when you are on a journey of stretching yourself and becoming successful, the nay Sayers, the people who put you down, the jokers who use their own insecurities to make sure they mock your achievements. This can be the close so called friend, family members, people who you love. If this is the case I am not saying for one minute that you should ban them from your life but a good piece of advice that I was given years ago was, "don't go as often and don't stay as long." Some people can suck all the strength from you by just being around them and it's not good to allow this to happen to your mind on a consistent basis.

"If you continue in the same old relationships with the same old Mind-Set, you will continue or return to the same old lifestyles."

There are old habits you have built up that are getting in your way; negative thinking, procrastination, comfort zones that are standing in the way of your success. Some of these feel good even though you know they are not good for you. Over eating and all the different choices of treats feel good when you're consuming them but if you're serious about becoming your ideal weight and staying healthy, then you must disassociate from them.

The past is the past and it should stay in the past. Let it go so that you can grow into your future.

8) **Depend on others for support:** This is one of the biggest mistakes people make when they want to change. I'm sure you think you can change everything in your life by yourself, but you can't. The quickest way to success is to find someone who is already achieving what it is you want to achieve and model them, their strategies, their habits, their ways of thinking, their success. How do you do that? Go ask them. Contact them and see if you can arrange a meeting with them. Offer to take them out to lunch or coffee and have a list of questions ready for them to answer. When you get the answers, if they are appropriate for what you are doing, then implement those ideas into place.

I have found that the most successful people are flattered when you ask for their help and they will help you in any way they can. I say most because I'm sure you will come across a few that are driven by arrogance and ego, who will snub you or ridicule you for even suggesting they help (as I have experienced in my career). You don't really need or want advice from anyone with this attitude.

There are enough successful people out there who will open up and give you advice. Many people will not take this step as due to fear, embarrassment or their pride gets in the way. They know it all and will figure it out on their own. It's amazing what happens when you have the courage to ask just one person for their advice. Two things happen; you walk away from that experience with so much pleasure and you find yourself on a mission to get as much information from as many people as possible. Well that's how it was for me.

I am the kind of person that when told how to do something I will just go out and have a go. Jump in with both feet and worry about getting it right along the way. I love a challenge. If I'm told I can't do something, then I must get it done. I'm a risk taker, a dreamer and I have never given up on something that I wanted to achieve.

Another great piece of advice I was given about people was this:

"The best way to impress people is to be impressed by them."

People love talking about themselves, especially successful people. They love sharing their stories and giving advice.

When you have the support of a few successful people, that you can turn to for advice, it makes the road to success a much easier road to travel. If you are the smartest or most successful person in your life, then you need to get a better quality of friends or associates.

How do you do this? Find new groups to join, set up a mastermind group or simply, as stated before, source out others that have already become successful in your chosen field and spend some time with them.

9) **Take time for yourself each day:** You must have quality time for yourself every single day that doesn't involved working on your plan. This is a crucial step in the achievement of your success. Most businessmen break down mentally and physically, long before their business breaks down. They fail because of their lack of "ME" time along the way; where they can recharge their batteries, unwind, get a new perspective and restart again with a refreshed mind and body.

One of the biggest mistakes most people make in life is not taking any quality time out of their day to unwind. Stress, anxiety and even depression is about being in your head too much and many times, making things worse than they actually are, through over analysing situations.

When you are over analysing and concentrating on the wrong things, then the physical body will reflect on those thoughts, so the mind and body are now on a downwards spiral of negativity. When I am working with clients who have stress related issues, this is the main cause in ninety-nine percent of the cases, no quality time for themselves. They dive into their goals 110% and leave no room to renewing their mind. Let me share with you a story that sums it up perfectly:

You must sharpen your axe

Once upon a time there was a very strong wood-cutter. He asked for a job from a timber merchant and he got it. The pay was very good and so was the work conditions, for that reason the wood-cutter was determined to do his very best. His boss gave him an axe and showed him the area in the forest where he was to work.

The first day the wood-cutter cut down eighteen trees. His boss was extremely impressed and said, "Well done. Keep it up. You are our best wood-cutter yet." Motivated by his boss's words, the wood-cutter tried even harder the next day, but he only cut down fifteen trees. The third day he tried even harder but only cut down ten trees, even though he was working just as hard as he did on day one.

Day after day the woodcutter cut down fewer and fewer trees. Knowing his potential and seeing how hard the man was working every day, the boss came to him and told him that he needed to be more productive to keep his job. The wood-cutter needed the job, so he tried harder and harder. He started working extra hours, during his lunch breaks and tea breaks, but still he could not cut down enough trees. "I must be losing my strength" the wood-cutter thought to himself. He worked over-time, but still it was not enough.

Eventually his boss came to him and told him he was fired. The wood-cutter was really upset, but he knew that he had worked as hard as he could and just did not have enough time to chop more trees. He sadly handed his axe back.

The boss took one look at the axe and asked, "When was the last time you sharpened this axe?"

"Sharpen my axe?" the wood-cutter replied. "I have never sharpened my axe. I have been too busy trying to cut down enough trees." Moral

of the story: Don't get too busy that you don't take the time to sharpen your axe.

You must take the time you need to relax, to think and meditate, to learn and grow. If you don't take the time to "sharpen your axe", you become dull, complacent and lose your effectiveness.

The worst excuse I hear each day when going through this with clients is, "I don't have the time." You must make time. Quality time for yourself is not something that should be over looked in your daily ritual for success. How you spend that quality time is just as important. It's not in front of the television with a glass of wine or two or three, getting out and taking a good walk is the best medicine of all.

I was never into walking I always preferred going to the gym and exercising which is also very effective, but when you are walking you can enjoy the peace and quiet to reflect on what you are doing and how to do it better. The mind can be allowed to switch off from the day and relax. It's amazing when the mind is relaxed how much you can learn and how many new ideas come to you.

When you are over-analysing things, you are not getting very far, there is too much going on. Get out into the countryside or down by the beach or somewhere where there is a bit of peace and quiet and you will be surprised how good this is for you and how much it helps your productivity.

So from today forward, take the time to sharpen your axe each day and if you don't have time, then make the time. There is no excuse.

10) Notice what is working and what is not: You must be totally certain of where you are going in life and what the target is.

How can you achieve something mentally or physically if you are all over the place and don't know what you want or where you're going in life?

If you are a follower of personal development speakers, coaches or trainers, I'm sure you have overheard the term, "know your outcome," to the point where you would think it is laboured. The fact is that most people don't know what they want out of life. Most people drift aimlessly through life hoping and wishing things will work out. They drift from one thing to another and wonder why they are not achieving the success they like to have. In reality they don't ever have a game plan. You need to have a game plan for your life if you are looking to go beyond what you are achieving right now and achieve success in a certain area. You need to continuously check that plan on a regular basis and see if what you are doing is taking you closer to where you want to be and if not, be able to adjust your course.

An airplane on its journey to a destination is off course most of the time, with the wind changing speeds and directions, but the pilot can navigate the plane back on course so it reaches the desired destination. You must be strong enough to stop what is not working in your life and make sure you adjust your plan to get you to where you are going.

When you are aimlessly drifting through life without a plan, then before you know it you end up somewhere you don't want to be and wondering how you got there, wondering how things got so bad. Just because you have been doing this for five, ten years or however long you have been drifting, doesn't mean to say you can't make the decision to stop doing what is not working for you and start doing something different that will get you the success that you want.

Being sick and tired of your life is not enough to change it. Knowing or even badly wanting to change is not even enough to change it. Getting pumped up and motivated about changing your life is not even enough to change it.

You have to have a strategy and put that strategy into place and implement it every single day for that change to become a reality. This all starts by having a game plan, a blueprint of what it is you want and where you are going.

If you are involved in sport or follow any kind of sport, you will know that before they start each match, each team will have a game plan. A boxer when fighting an opponent, will study that opponent; look for his weakness, find out his strengths and come up with his own game plan to win. "Stick to the game plan and you'll be fine" is a common instruction from a well-educated coach. Is your life not more important that a game of sport? If so, does it not seem ironic that we can put so much effort into preparing, developing and implementing a detailed game plan for a sporting event and we don't think of doing the same for our own lives?

"We only get to play this game of life one time, there's no going back to the parts we're not happy with and doing them again. So having a game plan for the rest

of your life should be just as big a part as living it."

So let's start the process of preparing our game plan and once we have it prepared we can then continue with the development stage.

The first step of our game plan and the process of renewing your mind is when you "set your mind" for change to take place in your life.

You set your mind to carry out something in your life just like you would set an alarm clock to wake you up in the morning. When you set that alarm clock you're pretty sure that the alarm will go off at that specific time in the morning.

Setting your mind for change means making a "quality decision" as to what you want and committing to the fulfilment of that decision.

Successful people in all walks of life become successful because they first set their mind for success. They program that success into their mind from the start.

They don't think to themselves, "How is this even possible?" "What if I fail?" What if someone makes fun of me and tells me I'm wasting my time?" NO! Firstly, they set their minds on what it is they want to achieve and then think, "How am I going to get from where I am right now to where I want to be?" "What is the first step I need to take?" They then go about designing a strategy which they put into place and follow on a daily basis. They first set their mind in alignment with that goal ahead, not on the problems that could come up along the way. Not the "What if's." So your first step is to make a quality decision of what it is you really want.

You don't set your mind according to circumstances.

You don't set your mind according to other people's opinion of how successful they think you will be.

You don't set your mind according to past fears or failures.

You set your mind on what it is exactly you would like to achieve and what it is that will take you there.

How you're going to get there, at this stage of the game plan has nothing to do with it, we will go into that part in a later chapter. Let's find out what it is you want before we move any further.

"Your goals are the road maps that guide you and show you what is possible in your life."

(Les Brown)

6

Goal Setting: Let's have some fun!

"The discipline you learn and character you build, from setting and achieving a goal, can be more valuable than the achievement of the goal itself."

Bo Bennett

When I was in sales I was introduced to books and tapes of motivational speakers such as Zig Ziglar, Brian Tracey, Jim Rohn, Earl Nightingale, Norman Vincent Peale, Les Brown, Tony Robbins and a few others. I thrived on this stuff because it did exactly what it said on the tin. It helped keep me motivated and focused on a daily basis. At that time, the information was the quality I needed to mentally stay focused each day. I have learned so much over the years from listening to other successful people who have mastered and crafted their profession. I can honestly say that within the last ten years, there probably hasn't been one single day that has gone by, with the exception of holidays, that I haven't listened, read something or watched something online to help keep my mind clean and free from negativity. I listen to this material when I feel a bit down or in challenging times. I listen to it when I'm in top form and need more inspiration. I have made this part of my daily rituals and it has become part of who I am. It's habit.

I take a lot from my experiences in life and always learn something with each experience. I keep journals so I can record information I hear from other speakers and coaches that has influence on me. I make sure I record them in my journal so I can go back time and time again to re-read or re-listen to the information. I have read several hundred books on personal development and I always read with a pen and a highlighter and mark, highlight and circle all the good stuff as I go through each book. If you were to take one of my many books off my book shelf in my office and flick through it, it is filled with various colours of highlighter, written quotes and passages as well as a list of books to read at the back of each book, that has been recommended by each author of the book I am reading at the time.

I believe this is such an important aspect of developing yourself because when you record the material you are reading or watching, listening to, it is stored information that you can revisit time and time again,

John's Story

One day a friend of mine called me up and asked if I could meet him for a coffee. He had gone through a messy divorce and he was at a stage where he didn't know if life was worth living (which were his words on the phone). I told him to come to my home and have a chat, as it would be a more private setting and he could open up if he felt the need.

As we sat and chatted and went through five or six cups of tea and coffee, he said to me, "You're into all this mumbo jumbo, wishy washy positive thinking stuff, what do you think I should do?"

When I'm working with clients, I would never try to direct them in a certain way by giving them my pennies worth of what I think they should do, that's not my job. My job is to elicit from my clients the answers they already know, by getting them to ask themselves better questions and focus on different meanings to the situations they are faced with. When they learn how to do this, they have the power to change anything in their lives. This power was always there, they just didn't know how to use it because they were focusing in the wrong direction, on the problem rather than the solution. So I did the same with him; I asked him if he was prepared to follow through on a task I set for him before I gave him my advice and he agreed to do so. I gave him three books that I thought could help him get into a better frame of mind so that he could make his own decisions, but from a different perspective. I then told him to go away and spend the next week reading the books. One book was written by Jim Rohn, one by Tony Robbins and the other was by Norman Vincent Peale. Reluctantly he took the books, as he was not a fan at all of this, "mumbo jumbo positive thinking stuff," as he always called it. But he promised to read the books and I knew the way he was feeling about himself, he would make some effort.

When a person gets to the stage in their life when they are sick and tired of being sick and tired, when enough is enough, then change can happen quickly, and my friend was at this stage.

A couple of days later, I was sitting at home and he turned up at the door, with all the books in his hand. He handed them back thanking me and asked if I had anymore.

Now I knew he couldn't have read all three books in one day as two of them were a pretty long read, so I confronted him about it. "I didn't have to read all of them; you have highlighted so much information and underlined so my things that I just read the parts you marked because I knew that if you had marked these parts, then they were the bits that stood out for you, so they were the important parts."

It was like a total transformation. We had another chat, went through another four or five cups of tea and coffee but this time the conversation was different. It was like sitting in front of a totally different person. He talked to me about his future and how he was re-joining the gym and starting to get fit again. He had an idea for a business that he was going to put into practice and he thanked me about a hundred times for helping him turn things around. He kept one of the books that had a structure within it of how to set your goals and plan your future and over the next few weeks he did just that and worked his plan. He now owns two businesses in recruitment and is happily married again to another lady he met about a year later. He has never been better. The ironic thing about the situation is that he is now a huge follower of all this, "mumbo jumbo, wishy washy positive thinking stuff." He has been to London on two separate occasions to take part in Tony Robbins weekends, seen Brian Tracy speak and is now involved in "Toastmasters," learning how to develop his skills in public speaking.

I share this story with you because it only takes one single book to change your life or one single idea to turn things around in your mind, no matter how bad you think things are. Changing your mind is only the first part; you have to have a plan of what you want to do next. The more detailed and concise that plan is, then the more likely you are to achieve it. So let's start on your plan for your future.

This chapter is all about goal setting. Getting your ideas from inside your head onto paper and creating a blue print of your life and your future. But I want to do it in a different way. I want to use this chapter to ignite your imagination, as if you were a kid again, as if you could have whatever you wanted.

For this part of the book you are going to need a pen and your journal. **You do have your journal, don't you?** We are going to go through this step by step and in detail so by the time you have finished this chapter, you will have a precise idea of what it is exactly you want, a timescale of how long it will take you to achieve it and a game plan of how to implement it.

This chapter will take you around thirty minutes to complete, so it's important to take the time to go through the follow exercises as directed. If you are reading this at a time when it isn't convenient, then put the book down and come back when you have the time. Don't simply read through this chapter, you need to get practically involved. Schedule a time when you have the time and do it in its entirety. You will enjoy the process and thank me afterwards.

I take no credit for the remainder of this chapter, as I am sharing with you a principle that I borrowed from the late Jim Rohn.

When I came across this idea of goal setting, I took the time and simply did what he suggested word for word. It had a profound impact on my life and I have been using it with my clients for years very successfully, so I see no reason to change or alter it for our purpose.

So let's get started:

I want you to first answer these questions and write down the answers in your journal.

Goal Setting Exercise: Let's play a Game:

Part 1: No Limitations

You are going to set your goals but you are going to set them in a different way. I want you to set them using your imagination, not logic and reason; we will go back to logic and reason as the exercise progresses.

Before we get into the question of goals, I want to you start off this exercise by writing down this question.

What are five things that you have accomplished in your life, up to now, that you are proud of?

Let's give yourself some credit for your past before you move onto your future. Really think about the question and don't move forward until you have written down five things. It can be small things, large things, simple things, but things that you have achieved that make you feel proud.

As you list these five things and look through them, what is it about accomplishing them that makes you feel proud?

Write the answers down underneath each of them. Be as precise as you can and really be truthful with yourself as to why these things stood out in your life over other things.

Let me tell you why I have included this at the start of our goal setting process.

Our sub-conscious mind is a pleasure seeker. It needs pleasure and recognition, but as adults we tend to put ourselves down and don't give ourselves enough credit for the things we have achieved in our life, sometimes to the point where we do it so much the mind automatically expects self-rejection. Someone trying to lose weight starts off well in the first week and then the second week is not as good. They get disheartened very easily and instead of having patience over a sustained period of time, they give up.

So look through the five things you have accomplished that you are proud of and give yourself a bit of credit for what you had done up until now. Give yourself a pat on the back for past achievements.

The next question is going to take some time because many of you reading through this may not have thought this far ahead.

What do you want in the next ten years?

Firstly, write the question down and then I want you to follow this simple rule when you write down your answers. The things you will write down are not what you think you can get, it is what you want if everything fell into place in your life if there were no limitations financially and you could have whatever you wanted in the next ten years.

What would that list be? I want you to list at least fifty things and list each item one under the other, not side by side. So it's one item per line (this is important) and go down until you have at least fifty items, even more if you can think of more.

Just let your dreams run free while answering the question.

Now remember it's not what you think you can get but what you would want if there are no limitations and you could have anything, in any area of your life.

Write down:

- small things,
- major things,
- thing's that may seem insignificant but you would have them anyway,
- places you would like to visit,
- what countries haven't you seen that you would like to visit,
- what cities excite you the most,

What kind of experiences would you like to have over the next ten years?

- parachute jump,
- walk the great wall of china,
- charity walks,
- act in a movie,
- play in a band,
- climb mountain Everest,

Remember there are no limitations. You can do or have

whatever you want or go wherever you want to go.

What would you like for your children?

What would you like for your partner?

Where would you like to take them?

What new skills would you like to learn over the next ten years?

- write a book,
- what courses you would like to take:
- a different profession you were always interested in,
- new habits you would like to acquire,
- play a musical instrument
- become fit.

Who would you like to meet over the next 10 years?

What famous person would you like to meet?

- pop star,
- movie star,
- prime minister or president,
- spiritual leader

What things interest you right now in your life that you would like to have time to do more of?

- Sport,

- business,
- travelling,

It's amazing when I go through this exercise how difficult it is for adults to get fifty things. Children, when asked to do this exercise, could fill two exercise books with the things they want. So use that imagination and really let yourself go crazy.

Maybe you would like a holiday home somewhere in a different part of the world. An apartment in:

- New York,
- California,
- Paris,
- London.

What investments would you have?

- properties,
- stocks
- bonds

How much money would you like to have in your bank account over the next ten years?

Where would you go on vacation each year?

- Australia,
- Bahamas,
- Hawaii
- China

- Mexico

What goals would you like to achieve in your career or business?

Would you, like to start up a new business?

If so, what would that business be?

What kind of business would excite you to be a part of?

Maybe you would like to do things for other people or help some kind of charitable organisation.

Would you like to speak a new language or a few languages? If so, which ones?

What skills would you like to teach your children?

What new skills would you like to learn yourself?

As you go through this list, think of:

- lifestyle goals,
- personal development goals,
- travel,
- personal possessions,
- Savings

Now as you come to the end of this part, I want you to put a star at the end of your list and this means that you can continue with the list over the next few days. If you take the time to think when going through this exercise, things will come to and as they do, add them to your list. The more you use your imagination the longer the list will become.

Goal Setting Process: Part 2

You should now have a list of goals, like a shopping list, that we can now work with and refine.

I want you to start at the top of your list, look down each item and give each item a number. The number being one, three, five or ten.

One equals one year

Three equals three years

Five equals five years and

Ten equals ten years

Go down the list and go over each item, putting a number for how long you think it would take you to achieve each item.

This doesn't have to be exact, just approximately.

Goal Setting Process: Part 3

Now as soon as you do that I want you to make a list of how many one's, three's, fives and ten's you have.

If you don't have any ten year goals it means that you are not stretching your mind far enough, so stop and think of some ten year goals that you could add to your list (you can add these over the next few days).

Goal Setting Process: Part 4

Now from your list, make out your top four one year goals. If you have a lot of one year goals, what are the most important to you or what would you prioritise over the others if you had the choice of only choosing four.

Next step is to take these four one year goals and write them on the top of a separate page; one page for each goal.

First of all, under each of these goals I want you to write down why they are a priority and how you would feel if you accomplished them within the next year. What would achieving them do for you personally, financially, emotionally, spiritually?

Now write down what is or has been stopping you from achieving these goals up until this moment. Write down all the obstacles or excuses or limiting beliefs or whatever it is you think that has got in the way of already having accomplished these goals. You need to be totally honest with yourself. If you look at one of the goals and you don't know what is stopping you then ask yourself this question, "If I did know what was stopping me, what would it be," this only has to be a line or two.

When you know what is stopping you, you can change it.

The next question, and probably the most important, to ask yourself, on each goal, is "Why"

Why do you want to achieve it?

What are your reasons?

Remember we talked about reasons in the last chapter and why they are so important.

When your why gets stronger and bigger, the how gets easier. W.I.I.F.M. What's in it for me? When you know why you are doing something and those why's are personal to you, it is those very "Why's" that will drive you in times of struggle.

So now you should have four goals that you have prioritised out of a list of fifty that you can start working on straight away.

You also have a list of other goals that you can set out to achieve over the next few years. You have set out a structure for the next ten years. You can go back to this list and add more or take some off that don't seem too important. If you took the time to write down fifty goals and you fine-tuned them over a few weeks and you ended up achieving only thirty of them over the next ten years, then how different would your life be.

Alternatively, if you spend the next ten years wishing and hoping things will work out and not even knowing what it is you want to achieve, where will you be in ten years' time?

It takes a bit of time to actually sit and go through this exercise and fine tune and re write some of the goals, but if you actually take the time to do it, it could change your entire life.

You should now have a list of one year goals you can get started on right away.

"Self-Mastery begins with mastering your thoughts; if you don't control what goes into your mind, you can't control what you do. Simple self-discipline enables you to condition your mind first and act afterwards."

(Napoleon Hill)

7

Conditioning Your Mind for Lasting Change.

"Your success in life ultimately arises

from the conditioning of your mind."

(Robert Herdman)

If you have taken the time to go through the goal setting exercise in the last chapter, you will be approaching this one with a fresh set of goals for your business and personal lives. These written goals will have a timescale and a plan to follow through. But in the past, how many times have you known what you wanted, believed it should be achievable, but cannot convince yourself that it is possible so you don't even try. You talk yourself right out of it for fear of failure, rejection or embarrassment of what other people might think.

I believe one of the most important aspects of achieving these new set of goals is programming them and conditioning them into your sub-conscious, through a process of renewing your mind.

Lasting change is not going to take place in your life without doing this.

With a new set of goals and the same old Mind-Set will eventually bring up the same barriers and limitations that have come up in the past. If you're in a brand new career, with the same old Mind-Set, your subconscious will eventually bring up fears and limiting beliefs from your past. If you're in a brand new relationship with similar jealousies and insecurities, it will only result in the same patterns as before.

Renewing your mind is a simple process of giving yourself new ideas on a regular basis; through repetition and conditioning these new ideas will become habit.

Setting your goals and having them on paper is only the first part of the process. When you take the time to renew your mind on a regular basis, you are growing mentally stronger and stronger each day and becoming the stronger version of yourself; through the challenges, despite the setbacks and no matter what other people think of you. This builds your character, develops your inner confidence and installs a new belief in yourself that you can and will achieve your list of goals because you have also develop the brand new Mind-Set to go along with them.

No matter what you are looking to accomplish in life; building a better relationship, starting a new business, learning a new skill, becoming financially independent or whatever success means to you, it is so important to develop the Mind-Set of the person you want to become along the way. This is how change lasts and success continues.

Developing an **"Unstoppable Mind-Set"** along the way to your success will get you to your destination quicker, helping you focus on the things you can change along the way and let go of the things you have no control of.

So developing that new Mind-Set is just as an important part of the process as the goal itself. If your Mind-Set stays the same, then your life stays the same. If your Mind-Set stays the same, then your marriage stays the same. If your Mind-Set stays the same, then your business stays the same.

And the truth is, if you have had any kind of life experience, you know that nothing ever stays the same. We are either growing or we are dying in life. We are progressing in what we are doing or we are dwindling and finding our way into our comfort zones.

Working on yourself on a daily basis is one of the most important gifts you can give to yourself. When you make the effort to put new ideas into your mind on a regular basis, like everything else, it becomes habit. It starts to run on auto pilot.

You start asking yourself better questions when faced with challenges. You become solution orientated instead of problem orientated. You start getting results, when before you would have given up.

Things start to turn around in your life because of that brand new Mind-Set.

When we come across a new idea or set a new set of goals, naturally we get pumped up and motivated. We feel excited as we think of what our future can be and what we can achieve.

However, getting pumped up and motivated in the moment, is not enough. We can all get motivated when we want to. It's staying motivated on a daily basis that is the key. It's great when you're planning a new venture and feel good about it, but what about when you start to implement that plan and you start running into obstacles, because you will. What about next week, or next month or six months down the line; when you go back into your world and all the same subconscious patterns of the old Mind-Set are still there.

This is where conditioning comes in. You need to be in the position of improving your game all the time.

Some people will say to me, "Oh I tried all that positive stuff once before and it didn't work for me," and I always remind them of a quote from the great motivational speaker and sales trainer, Zig Ziglar;

"People often say to me that motivation doesn't last; well neither does bathing, that's why we recommend it each day."

Being successful in life is a discipline, it's about doing the right things every day. When you go through life's journey you are going to come across many challenges in your quest for success. You are always faced with the right way or the easy way but you always have a choice as to which path to take.

Renewing your mind is not a one-time event; when things crash, you need a pick me up to get you back on track again. Renewing your mind should be an ongoing endeavour. You're going to have to enter into training, just like an athlete trains for an event, until new thoughts become conditioned into your sub-conscious mind and run automatically.

Am I saying that when you renew your mind you're never going to have any problems again? Not at all! Is it going to be easy? No it's not!

- Because you're still going to have those days when you feel like staying in bed that extra hour or two, but when you start the process of renewing your mind and because of that new Mind-Set, you will get yourself out of bed and you will make the decision to **Keep Moving Forward.**
- You may still find yourself in situations where nothing seems to be going right and you feel so overwhelmed that you just want to cry: but when you continue the process of renewing your mind and because of that new Mind-Set, you have your cry, you will get over yourself and you will make the decision to **Keep Moving Forward.**
- Your pride may get hurt along the way to success, but when you continue the process of renewing your mind and because of that new Mind-Set, you will learn how to swallow your pride, you will make the decision to **Keep Moving Forward.**
- You may have to do things that you don't want to do, but when you continue the process of

renewing your mind and because of that new Mind-Set you get yourself a backbone instead of a wishbone and you will make the decision to **Keep Moving Forward.**

- Sometimes your steps are going to be small and you may not feel as if you're getting anywhere, but that's ok. Why? Because when you continue the process of renewing your mind and because of that new Mind-Set, you will realise that you are still on track and you will make the decision to **Keep Moving Forward.**

- You might have someone put you down or try to stamp on your dreams, but when you continue the process of renewing your mind and because of that new Mind-Set, you build a bridge, get over it and you will make the decision to **Keep Moving Forward.**

- Your heart may become heavy along the way on your journey to success, but when you continue the process of renewing your mind and because of that new Mind-Set: you are able to take control of your emotions on a daily basis and you will make the decision to **Keep Moving forward.**

- And then after a while you find yourself getting into a certain rhythm, you see things moving quicker and you realise you are fulfilling your life's purpose. No matter what happened along the way, because you made the decision to continue the process of renewing your mind and because of that new Mind-Set, you decided to pick yourself up time and time again and you made the decision each time you were faced with a challenge along the way to **Keep Moving forward.**

You now feel more confident, you believe in yourself and what you are doing because you have developed what I call **"An Unstoppable Mind-Set."** When you develop an unstoppable Mind-Set, nothing and no one can stop you from going from where you are in your life right now to where you want to be.

That's the difference between successful people and people who just get by in life.

How to develop "An Unstoppable Mind-Set"

The first step in developing that unstoppable Mind-Set is choosing what you are allowing into your mind on a daily basis. Remember what you allow to happen to yourself on a daily basis, is what will ultimately continue in your life.

The things that you allow to enter into your mind consistently will have a huge effect on how you think, how you feel and how you behave.

There is an old Cherokee story about a tribal elder, who is teaching his grandson about life. "A fight goes on inside of me" he says to the boy. "It is a fight between two wolves. One is evil: he is anger, envy, sorry, regret, guilt, depression, fear, greed, arrogance, self-pity, resentment, inferiority, lies, false pride, superiority, and ego. The other is good: He is joy, happiness, peace, love, hope, serenity, humility, kindness, benevolence, empathy, generosity, truth, compassion and faith. This same fight goes on inside of you and inside every other person too."

The grandson thought about it for a minute and then asked his grandfather, "Which wolf will win?"

The old Cherokee simply replied, "Which ever one you feed the most."

So as you are reading through this let me ask you a few questions:

What are you feeding into your mind on a daily basis at this present time? Is it constructive or destructive?

How are you making yourself feel each day, from when you get up in the morning until you retire at night?

You are there twenty-four hours a day, seven days a week, three hundred and sixty-five days a year and you and you alone have the power to make yourself feel successful, motivated, inspired amazing, happy and contented or something entirely different.

"Whether you think you can or you think you can't, either way, you're right."

(Henry Ford)

When you continue to tell yourself that you can't do something or that it is impossible or even worse, you see yourself in your mind already failing even before you make an attempt. You are using your imagination to create that very image you fear. That image, through repetition, becomes stored in your sub-conscious mind and this becomes your reality. You start acting out on that reality as if it were true. You start coming up with all the reasons why it can't be done and you come up with ways of justifying these reasons to yourself. Another goal or dream slips through your fingers.

When you start a process of renewing your mind; talking to yourself differently, seeing yourself achieving those goals, you are sending new information to our subconscious mind. Through repetition, this starts to become your reality, and you act out on that reality.

When you start seeing yourself differently in your mind it generates new feelings in your body. How you make yourself feel on a daily basis will determine how successful you will become on a daily basis.

Things happen to you when you reprogram your mind each day. You start moving forward instead of backward in your life. You stop making excuses because you have taken back control and you no longer let the negative opinions of others influence your world.

Igniting your Powerful imagination

Before we get into the next chapter, let me give you a heads up on how the imagination works and how to use it effectively.

Most of the time we pre-dominantly think in pictures. If I ask you to think of the colour of your front door, you will think of a picture in your mind of the colour. Close your eyes and do it now. Think of the colour of your front door and see that picture. Seeing your goal in your mind through a process of creative visualisation is simply picturing yourself already achieving it and reinforcing that goal through repetition as you move toward it.

How it works:

The sub-conscious cannot distinguish between an image that is real or imaginary. Visualising your goals each day gives your mind a clear direction of where you want to go in life. Once you impress that image upon the sub-conscious through repetition, you are giving your reticular activating system a direction of what to focus and it will help bring you closer to your goal.

Reticular Activating System or (RAC)

The reticular activating system or RAS for short is composed of several neuronal circuits connecting the brainstem to the cortex part of your brain. Your reticular activating system acts as a filter against all the data and information that is around us. There is so much information coming to us at any one time that your brain cannot take everything in so your RAC filter only lets things through that it thinks is important. It knows how to do this by picking up what you "focus on" most. This is universal and works every time. Have you ever noticed that people who continually say, "I'm not very confident" are not confident people? People who tell themselves, "I can never lose weight" actually never lose weight. What you focus on consistently you manifest in your life, because your RAC will show you things to prove that this is true for you. The more proof you see, the more you start to believe that this is true and then this becomes your reality. But when you start using the power of creative visualisation and positive self-talk, your RAC will start to show you things to prove that your new belief is true for you.

"The greatest achievement in life is to have the ability to create the world around you so that it matches the dreams in your head."

(Mike Dillon-Entrepreneur)

8

It All Starts With a Vision. What's Yours?

"The man who has no imagination, has no wings."

(Muhammad Ali)

What if we could plan our success in our mind and by impressing our success with clarity, simply by using our imagination and pretending, we could speed up that process? These tools exist and are collectively called "Creative Visualisation." Creative visualisation has been used by all the great achievers throughout the world of business, sport and science for hundreds of years.

Let me share with you two very different examples that bring to light the power of creative visualisation and how it can transform a person's life.

"Logic will get you from A to B. Imagination will take you everywhere." (Albert Einstein)

The Miracle Man: Morris E. Goodman.

Morris E. Goodman is one of the most famous and classic examples of the phenomenal effects of visualisation. Goodman proved that by the power of the human mind and dedication, one can do the impossible.

His story starts in 1981 when the plane he was flying crashed. The impact was devastating. He wound up in the hospital completely paralysed. The doctors' prognosis was poor and they told him that he would be a vegetable for the rest of his life. His diaphragm and lungs were so badly damaged that he had to be hooked to a volume respirator to maintain airway circulation. Many people in his condition might have wondered what they could really amount to when all they could do was blink their eyes. But being the fighter that he is, Goodman summoned all his strength and courage and through the use of the alphabet and eye blinking, told the nurse that he would walk out of the hospital on Christmas day. While the medical team commended his fighting spirit, they did not really believe that he could do it.

Day in and day out, Goodman visualised how he would be walking out of the hospital on his own two feet. He vividly imagined the details and the shocked faces of the people in the hospital, medical practitioners and patients alike.

One day, Goodman felt the sudden urge to breathe on his own. With all his might, he inhaled deeply. From then on, his progress amazed the people who knew his story. His full recovery was splashed on every tabloid and newspaper in town.

Today, he is a highly sought-after speaker who travels around the world sharing his success story. He encourages people to believe that no matter what hand life deals them, they can still accomplish their goals, achieve happiness and have contentment in their hearts. His favourite saying, **"man becomes what he thinks about,"** *is what he leaves his audience to ponder on just before leaving the stage.*

Morris Goodman was one of the stars of the film "The Secret." He is truly a powerful example of the power of the human mind and what can be achieved by simply impressing what you want into your sub-conscious each day, as a part of the transformation process.

The second story I want to share with you is a more recent achievement that has been broadcast throughout the world recently.

The Mind of a Champion

In case you have been on another planet over the last few months, Conor McGregor is a rising Irish MMA fighter who on 12th December 2015 knocked out defending UFC champion Jose Aldo in just thirteen seconds. Aldo previously had been undefeated in ten years. The reason I have included Conor in this book, is not so much to share with you his story of success, as this has been broadcast repeatedly throughout the media, but because of the great dedication he has to his mental belief and his continuous dedication to visualisation. These are some of the quotes that have come from McGregor:

"Knowing that I had that mentality of already winning the championship, even before I won it, always gave me the confidence I needed when I got into the cage, every fight leading up to the championship."

"I've already visualised being a champion so I know it will come to pass."

"I already know what that championship belt feels like wrapped around my waist because I have visualised it so many times and each time I visualise it, I get that feeling, so when I do win that belt that feeling will be familiar."

"There is no opponent in front of me, I am against myself in there and I have already won because I visualise it over and over."

"I believe in myself so much that nothing is going to stop me: but I couldn't have had this belief, if I didn't see it in my mind every day over and over."

"…. if I didn't it wouldn't have happened. I had to believe it, I had to have faith in it and I had to see it in my mind…"

"If you have a clear and concise picture, in your mind of what is going to happen and a clear belief in that picture then it will happen, no matter what."

"Once you visualise it, it is destined to happen, nothing can stop it."

"I truly believe that to be at the pinnacle of any game or whatever you do in life, you have got to be a little bit gone, you have got to be almost insane to your craft, seeing it in your mind long before it happens and not a lot of people can understand that."

McGregor is the perfect example of the power of creative visualisation

As I said earlier being successful at anything in life is a very deliberate process. The mind and the body are interlinked and many people have compared the mind as the "control panel" of your system. If you look at high achievers in any profession I'm sure you will see that they were successful long before they actually achieved that success in its physical application as a result of what they had been programming into their mind for years.

The great and the most exciting thing about this process is that anyone can do it. It's universal, without exception and can be started at any stage. It doesn't matter what age you are or how many times you have failed in something before. It's about starting a new process with your mind and developing that process until it becomes, sound familiar.

Visualisation is not something you do just one time and expect miracles to happen. It's not something you try out for a week or so and "hope" things work out. It's a process where you must put 100% of yourself into it. You must have faith in something you have not yet achieved and see that achievement in your mind, using your imagination with the utmost faith and conviction that it will come to pass. This is why it is hard to comprehend for most people and why only a chosen few will do it.

What is Creative Visualisation

Creative Visualisation is simply a way of using your imagination. What you are really doing, if you break it down, is pretending, just like you were a young child, allowing that pretence to guide you in the direction of your goals. Imagination to adults is like pretend to children. Pretend to children is a word that means make believe.

But if you look at the word pretend and the word intent, they are connected. Before you get your intention, you have got to see it already happening in your mind. You have got to make believe that it is happening in your mind's eye.

You have got to have a clear vision of what you want to create and what you want your life to be about.

When you are continually picturing, imagining and visualising that you are already there in your mind, the most interesting things happen in your life. The people, places, things events and opportunities start to show up in your life.

So I want to take you on a simple experiment of visualisation, and remember visualisation is simply using your imagination

As this is an experiment and we are just pretending there is no right or wrong, there is only what you allow to happen in your own mind, everyone's experience will be totally different. Read through this exercise a few times before you practically do it to familiarise yourself with the process. Remember this is your imagination and you can do whatever you want, you are just making it up, so really have a go at this next exercise, with that pretence of the little kid you once were.

I also want to point out to you that if you just read through this and don't follow through on the exercise, then nothing will happen at all.

Exercise: Visualising Your Success

Stop for a moment right now and imagine what it would be like to have already achieved the success you want in your life?

What would it be like if you woke up one morning and a miracle had happened: Your life had become exactly what you wanted it to be in every area?

Do it now, close your eyes for me and pretend and vividly imagine it in your mind.

How would you know that that miracle had taken place?

What would you see?

What would you hear?

How would you feel inside?

What changes would have happened in your life?

In your career:

In your relationships:

In your finances:

In your health:

Whatever those changes would be for you:

How would you know that your life had changed?

What would be different?

Now take a deep breath all the way in and as you exhale,

simply using your imagination, I want you to see your life in your mind's eye in your future and how your life is totally different.

You have achieved all the things you wanted to change and using all your senses I want you to:

See what you see,

Hear what you hear and,

Feel how it feels now you have achieved these things in your life.

Take a deep breath in, and as you exhale this time, I want you to imagine the good feeling that you're experiencing right now flowing down through every muscle and nerve and fibre of your body.

Take in another deep breath and once again just imagine this good feeling flowing through every muscle and nerve and fibre of your body once again.

Positive Mental Expectancy

How did you do in this exercise? If you are new to all this stuff then it can seem a bit silly, but there are too many examples through the history of human success stories to brush of visualisation as nonsense or wishy washy mumbo jumbo, as my friend described it in an earlier chapter.

Like anything else we do for the first time, we are not too good at it. It takes practice, repetition and impressing it upon your sub-conscious mind often enough that you can actually link the pictures to the physical feelings, but it is achievable to anyone. There is one more ingredient required to complete the process though.

One of the great assets that all great achievers have is that they live in a Mind-Set of expectancy. They just know they will achieve their success. They expect to be successful. Do they have any guarantees? No. They usually come up against so many defeats and failures along the way, looking back, in many cases it's hard to comprehend why they stuck it out to the end. The temptation to quit, at times, was so strong. One of the commonalities of all successful people is that they just expect to succeed. They have what I call a "Positive Mental Expectancy". There is no doubt in their mind and this expectancy is the fuel and the electricity that ignites those pictures in their mind, making the process of creative visualisation so real. When you start seeing yourself differently in your mind, it generates new feelings in your body and how you make yourself feel will determine how successful you will become on a daily basis.

What stops people from having a positive mental expectancy?

1) Self-doubt, almost always based on previous experiences – experiences of not getting what you want, needless to say.

2) Fear, which distracts you from certainty and sets up doubt.

3) And losing focus; taking your mind off the objective you want and forgetting that you are expecting it to happen.

This is where combining creative visualisation with a positive mental expectancy can make all the difference and certainly the difference in those who succeed and those who don't follow through.

6 steps to begin using Creative Visualisation

Step 1: Set the mood: Relaxation is the key to learning and as human beings we learn best when we are relaxed and focused. So if you are starting creative visualisation for the first time I suggest you set some time aside for your first experience and get yourself into a comfortable and relaxed setting. Find a place where you won't be disturbed and can be comfortable for the duration of the process. You might prefer to be lying or sitting in a peaceful area or soaking in a hot bath or listening to mellow instrumental music. Remember the time you allocate to this process each day, the more effective it will be.

Step 2: Relax your mind by getting into a meditative state: I tend to find visualisation to be most intense and meaningful if you take the time to do a straightforward meditative exercise before you begin. This can simply be to take some deep breathes in and out and to focus on your mind and body, relaxing and unwinding.

Step 3: Visualise Your Goal: Once you feel relaxed, then create a picture in your mind of your goal as if you have already achieved it. See it as if you are running a movie in your mind. The key is to get all you other sense involved; see what you see, hear what is going on and feel in your nervous system what it feels like to have achieved this goal. Imagine you had a remote control and you could turn up the volume, make the images brighter and make those feelings as intense as you can to the extent you can feel a state change in your body. Make the environment around that goal in your mind as realistic as possible, as you experience not just the sights but also the sounds, scents and sensations associated with your goal.

Step 4: Revisit the feelings throughout your day to strengthen the process: Although the most important part of creative visualisation is the process described in step three, you are more likely to see your goals manifest in your life if you allow your visualisation experiences to influence the rest of your day. Try to hold onto the feelings of pride, happiness, confidence and peace that you experience when you picture your goal and repeatedly affirm your belief that you will soon attract the things you yearn for.

Step 5: Repetition through Mental Rehearsal: To become good at something it takes practice and this process is no different. Ideally, you should make creative visualisation a daily part of your life. To start off you should set aside a specific time for the visualisation (such as a fifteen-minute period before going to sleep or first thing in the morning when you awaken), but the most important thing is that you maintain your ritual of visualising your goal until you obtain what you want in your life.

Step 6: Work hard each day toward your goal: Although creative visualiation is incredibly powerful and can certainly play a huge role in allowing you to develop the life you've always wanted, you cannot achieve your goal if you do not take practical action each day, so you must also take concrete steps towards your goals. We will go through this step in detail in the final part of this book.

Whatever your thoughts on creative visualisation up until now is not important because this book is helping you develop new habits and if your life is not working the way you want it to and you are working hard each day, then maybe this is the missing ingredient. Look at all the great successes that you admire and I'm sure if you look how they become successful, there was some sort of visualisation process incorporated in their success.

In the world of business and sport there are too many examples of high achievers using creative visualisation for it to be dismissed.

Before we go onto the third principle of success there is one more element I want to cover, that I feel is of great importance, and that is the use of "Power Words".

"Words can inspire you:

Words can destroy you.

Choose yours well."

(Robin Sharma)

9

Developing a New Vocabulary

"I Am: Two of the most important words.

Because what you put after them shapes your reality."

(Joel Osteen)

Power Words that Control Us

How we talk to ourselves basis has an enormous effect on what actions we will take on a daily basis. The words you use internally is your ability to represent, to yourself what is happening on the outside world.

There are roughly over one million words in the English language but generally most people tend to use the same habitual words to describe their experiences of life. If you only use a small handful of words to describe your life experiences, then you are limiting yourself and containing yourself within the emotions these words elicit. Human beings tend to use certain words on a regular basis to describe how they feel, but through time, these words become patterned

I call these words Power **Words** because they have the power to change your state of mind, in a split second. These words become anchors to the emotional states they elicit and when we habitually use these words, the emotions become anchored into our nervous system and run automatically.

If your experience of life is just, "OK, "then this is the label you put on it. Having an "OK" day is different from having "An Amazing day".

If you think about the beliefs, you have in life; beliefs start off as a series of words that become habit. If we change one simple word, we can literally change our beliefs. Let me give you a simple example the two most common words people use on a daily basis.

If you are faced with a new situation in life and you tell yourself, "I Can't do this," then this will have an effect on how you feel. How you feel, will then effect how you behave in that situation and how you behave will automatically effect what kind of action you will take. The action you take will then determine how you move forward in that situation. If you have started with telling yourself, "I can't do this, "then this will leave an impression on your sub-conscious mind. When you are faced with that situation a number of times and your thought process is "I Can't, "then this becomes a belief and you act on that belief as if it is reality, when in actual fact it is not. It is only your reality that was started and reinforced with two simple words, "I Can't."

If you go back to that situation and you tell yourself, "I Can "or "I Will "then this simple change in vocabulary will change the way you feel. When you feel different you behave differently and this will also affect what actions you take. A simple shift in your vocabulary can alter your course in life.

I know this sounds simplistic but if you are in a situation where you feel less than resourceful, then to change how you feel you must start somewhere and where better to start, than by developing some new empowering vocabulary.

Michael's Story

Michael was recommended to come and see me as he was suffering from depression ". As he came in to my office I could see, before he even spoke, he was feeling pretty miserable as his body language reflected his mood. As he sat in my "Hypnosis Chair "as I call it, I asked him to give me in his own words, a thumb nail sketch of what had brought him to see me. Before he spoke I asked if I had his permission to write a few notes, which he agreed to. As he spoke, I put to paper the words he was using that described his experiences. This is a short account of the first couple of minutes of his conversation,

*My life is a total **mess** at the minute. I have been **suffering** from **depression** for a couple of years now and at the minute I feel so **down**. I have felt really **down** for quite a while. Sometimes I'm fine but most of the time I just feel **down and depressed. Life is hard.** I try to do my best but it's hard when you're **feeling down all the time.** I know I have a great family and they do what they can for me but when your **feel so low all the time…. have you ever felt down? I'm sure you have, it's not a nice feeling but I feel like this all the time….** It's as if*

*I'm trapped in a **dark place** and **I can't seem to get free.** **Life sucks** to be honest and **I don't know what to do.***

Habitual words become patterned and if you only have one or two words for each experience in life, this becomes logged into your nervous system.

When we think of power words we normally associate words that are positive or empowering. However, many people use strong negative words which also have the power to change how you feel instantly. A lot of people will have very intense negative words and very neutral or week words to describe positive experiences. Words such as overwhelmed, pissed off, depressed, overpowering, out of control, down, disappointed, agitated, stressed, despair, apprehensive, distressed, doomed, failure, traumatised etc. When these words are used on a regular basis the feeling associated with it will be experiences as well.

These negative power words can really affect everything we do on a daily basis and we use these words as labels. These labels then become the experience.

We can also become conditioned into using very neutral words to describe the positive experiences in life.

Our goal in life should be to have more pleasurable experiences than painful ones, but if we use phrases such as, "just ok," "not too bad," "could be better," to describe our daily experiences, how can we truly appreciate the experiences that life gives us. When we become so negative, neutral or flat in our self-talk, we suck out the pleasure of our experiences.

The alarm clock goes off and Jane leans over to hit the snooze button for the third time. "Not **another Monday** "*she thinks to herself.* "I **hate** *Monday's; it must be the* **worst day** *of the week. I suppose I'll have to* **drag myself** *out of bed before I'm late for work yet again.* "*She gets out of bed and draws the bedroom curtains to be greeted with the heavy rain, beating on the outside of the bedroom window.* "*This weather is* **so depressing. I can't even be bothered** *with work today,* "*she tells herself.* "*I'm* **not feeling the best** *to be honest. I wonder if I'm* **coming down** *with something. I* **absolutely hate** *having the flu. I'll* **probably be a zombie by lunchtime.** *I'm supposed to go to the gym tonight but there's no point* **now that I'm sick."**

"**I'm the worst sufferer in the world** *and I've no sick days left in work. If anyone gets on the* **wrong side of me** *today God help them.* **I hate my life.** *Why does* **nothing good** *ever happen to me?* **I must be the unluckiest person in the whole world.** *I think I'll go make myself some coffee to see if this will make me feel any better.* "

Who has been here in some shape or form?

The habitual words we use on a daily basis shape our entire lives.

What are some of the habitual words you may use that have a negative effect in your life?

Remember your experience of life is determined by:

> a) the way you talk to yourself and the words you use and
>
> b) the way you represent things to yourself.

When you expand your vocabulary, you expand the quality

of your experiences and you therefore expand the quality of your life.

What would happen if you took certain habitual negative words out of your vocabulary and decided not to use them anymore? Would the feeling that is attached to them also disappear? If you removed certain words altogether then you would have no way to experience it.

By replacing these negative words with more empowering alternative and developing new triggers that fire off new meanings, you are transforming your experiences by feeling something entirely different.

When was the last time you got out of bed and said to yourself?

"Something amazing is going to happen to me today "

"Today is going to be such a great day for me "

" This day will bring so much pleasure with it "

Sounds corny, right! But what if you tried it for a few weeks and really did it with intent, I am totally convinced that you would feel different in a few weeks' time. Come on, this is all about building new habits so give it a go, no one will even know except you. Let me give you a few choices to make your experience more empowering.

There are so many words that you can use on a daily basis that can make you instantly feel good. Words like, amazing, fantastic, motivated, super, exceptional, extraordinary, great and terrific.

Look up the dictionary or a thesaurus and see what kind of

words you can come up with. I find it works better when you use words that are not in your vocabulary right now, it's more fun.

Here is a list of a few more that I have included that you can use.

Optimistic	Amazing	Cheerful	Inspired
Determined	Dynamic	Impulsive	Blessed
Fortunate	Confident	Delightful	Empowered
Vibrant	Awesome	Special	Grateful
Ecstatic	Radiant	Vivacious	Exuberant

Take the word, "Spectacular "for instance. Imagine how you would feel if you felt spectacular. Imagine it for a second. Close your eyes, take a deep breath in and as you exhale tell yourself, "I feel absolutely spectacular "and notice what feelings come up. Do you feel silly, amused, or a bit weird because it's the first time you have ever done this? Remember this is your imagination and you can do whatever you want with your imagination.

I can guarantee you one thing; that if you practiced this one sentence each day, closed your eyes and said, "I feel absolutely spectacular "for a period of time, you would not feel down or depressed or angry.

Here's a fun exercise I teach in my workshops and it has great results in helping people change their state of mind instantly. It is also great fun to do:

Instant "Feel Good Factor "exercise: Just for Fun

Take this one sentence:

" I feel absolutely fantastic, but I'll get better. "

Read this over a few times to get the meaning of it. Now this is how you use it.

When you meet someone and they ask you how you feel, your answer is, "I feel absolutely fantastic, but I'll get better. "

Even if you don't feel fantastic, I promise you, the look on the other person's face will instantly make you laugh and you will instantly feel better.

Some of the reactions that I have got from people when I have said this have been classic. Some people look at you as if you're from another planet, some people instantly finish the conversation and move on as quickly as they can. Some people burst into fits of laughter at even the thought of what you have said.

This exercise is so simple and it is so much fun, I use it everywhere.

Different words automatically generate different feelings and the trick here is to anchor the new power words with the feelings they elicit.

Speaking with power, both on the inside and out, also creates a sense of accountability and commitment to get the best from yourself and others. Challenge yourself to consciously avoid using words that are power draining. These words sap energy and commitment from your interactions, and ultimately, your actions.

What if you were to replace some of your negative habitual words with some really humorous or funny words that when you said them, you just couldn't take it seriously? e.g. "I'm so depressed," replacing this with, "I'm so bumfuzzled "Bumfuzzled is a word that means flustered. How could you feel anything other than humorous if you replaced the two words? Let me give you a few more words that you can use in the next exercise.

Jaunty	Perky	Pooped	Bouncy
Insouciant	Bushy-tailed	Sweezy	Jocose
Peeved	Vexed	Fruitful	Hulked

Remember the key to doing this is to find out what negative habitual words you are using and find out something that is of similar meaning but sounds totally weird, funny or just make something up. The aim is to break the pattern and get the new word to disassociate you from the habitual emotion, replacing it with a more empowering emotion.

At the end of this chapter I have come up with an exercise to help you break the old pattern of negative power words and replace them with a more humorous alternative.

Before you go through the exercise I want you to come up with three words that you use habitually to describe the negative emotions you feel on a daily basis. Maybe you say things like, "I feel so down or depressed "or "I hate this "or "Life sucks." Take some time and remember some of the negative things you would repeatedly say to yourself daily.

When you have remembered these words, I want you to come up with three alternatives that are words you would never use but will make the situation funny. Three funny words that when replaced in those situations, will make you feel different. E.g. "I'm really angry" to "I'm really pooped," I'm so depressed" to "I'm so boogled." The sillier the word, the more it will break the pattern. The word doesn't even have to be a real word, you can make it up. The idea here is to break the old pattern; so the funnier or more outrageous the word the more it will do the job.

Spend a bit of time on this and write down as many funny words as you can to replace the old situations. I have given you a few examples below.

Remember this is all a bit of fun but when you start using it, it has so much power in changing how you feel from day to day. And once again remember, it only works if you actually practice it.

Have a go at this next exercise, read through it first a few times and then practically go through the content of the steps involved.

Changing your vocabulary exercise.

Take in a deep breath in, and as you exhale close your eyes...

1) *Think of a negative word that you would use habitually that makes you feel worse.*

2) *As you think about it for a second, remember how it makes you feel.*

3) *Think of a place where that emotion would normally come up.*

4) *Now imagine going into that situation in your mind.*

5) *As you go into that situation, say the funny alternative word and see yourself smile, finding the alternative funny. Make the situation like a cartoon, where everything is animated. Say the alternative word in a cartoon voice, like Micky Mouse, Tweety Bird or your favourite cartoon character. See what you see, hear what you hear and let that feeling come up in place of the old negative feeling. Actually smile while you are going through this exercise and anchor that good feeling inside.*

6) *Now make it happen in your mind really quickly. Think of a few other situations where you would normally get upset and say the alternative words you have. Go through the same process, animate the scene in your mind, hear yourself saying the word in your favourite cartoon voice and feel good whilst you are doing it. See what you see, hear what you hear and actually smile as you are going through this mental rehearsal.*

7) *See yourself in all situations where you would have felt that old feeling but with the new behaviour.*

8) *In your mind see it working out, where you see it better for you and people are responding better.*

9) *In your mind run five or six scenarios. The key to doing this is speed and emotion; increase the emotional intensity each time breaking the old pattern and reinforce this new pattern.*

10) *Each time you do it, make it more outrageous or funny some way. Think of where would be the best places to use this new behaviour.*

11) *Before you open your eyes, ask your sub-conscious mind if it will accept this new pattern for the next seven days and help you to use it in these situations and see if it works.*

12) *Practice this as much as you can.*

A: Action

C: Changes

T: Things

Part 3

Putting on your own
C.A.P

C.ontinuous

A.ction

P.lan

"You are what you do, not what you say you'll do."
(C.G. Jung)

10

The Missing Ingredient: Deliberate Action

"Knowing is not enough,

We Must Apply.

Willing is not enough.

We Must Do.

(Bruce Lee)

Once upon a time a man was walking through a forest when he saw a crippled fox. "I wonder how it manages to feed itself," he thought.

At that moment, a tiger approached, carrying its prey in its mouth. The tiger ate its fill and left what remained for the fox.

"If God helps the fox, he will help me too," the man thought. He went back home, shut himself up in his house and waited for the heavens to bring him food.

Nothing happened.

He lay there in bed waiting for God to provide for him as he had for the fox, but instead he just starved.

Just when he was becoming almost too weak to go out and work, an angel appeared.

"Why did you decide to imitate the crippled fox?" asked the angel. "God has given you gifts and abilities to contribute to the world and make a living, while looking after the crippled foxes of the world. Get out of bed, pick up your tools and follow the way of the tiger!"

Let me ask you a question; which one are you, the fox or the tiger?

Are you sitting around waiting for things to happen? If you are, let me tell you; they're not going to! You're going to starve.

All successful people in life; the visualisers, the high achievers, the leaders, are all massive action takers. They know that if they want something they have to step up and make it happen by taking action.

They have taken responsible for their own lives and their success. They renew their mind on a regular basis and visualise themselves already in the possession of what they want. One hundred percent of all high achievers know that without taking continuous action everything else is a waste of time.

It's good to create your vision board and see yourself in the possession of nice things in your mind. It's good to get all pumped up and motivated by going to a conference and listening to great speakers. It's good to make a list of goals to achieve over the next five and ten years. Whilst you are doing all of this, it will make you feel good in the moment.

Getting up off your backside and actually doing something every day, to make all those things become reality, is what it's all about. **ACTION=RESULTS.**

In my opinion this is the main ingredient that separates successful people from the rest of society.

There is no other way. There are no short cuts and there are no magic formulas that will get you there if the action part is missing.

Becoming successful at any thing in life is a very deliberate process, as we have discussed in earlier chapter. The main key that has to be turned in the open door for success is taking "Deliberate Action."

Deliberate action is totally different from taking any old action, which you take simply to make yourself look busy. Deliberate action is structured and on purpose. It is planned and set so that you know that with each piece of action you take, it will move you one step forward each time in the achievement of your goal. Let me explain:

Don't confuse activity with accomplishment.

How many days have you wasted checking through emails, going through Facebook, listening to video clips on YouTube and all the while nothing is getting accomplished? If you start your day at 8pm and you finish at 5pm it means absolutely nothing. It's just a timescale throughout the day. What progress you have made throughout those hours is the only thing that matters.

I remember listening to Jim Rohn on YouTube and he asked the question, "Are you majoring in minor things" and I've used this ever since. I typed it out in a word document on my computer, printed it out and put it up on the wall above my computer screen. Every time I go onto the computer this helps me focus on what I need to do by taking deliberate action and not get lost in the sea of nonsense that is on the internet.

Just because you're busy throughout the day it doesn't mean you accomplish the major things you need to get done. Activity and accomplishment are totally different.

I want to spend the last few chapters of this book setting out a structure you can use on a daily basis; a continuous action plan, that if you put into place will bring you to your goals by implementing consistency and repetition, therefore becoming a person of action every day.

Remember this; when you want to achieve something in your life that you haven't achieved up until now, your life MUST become different and you MUST be prepared to change. If you really want to become your ideal weight then eating better, exercising regularly, getting better sleep and drinking plenty of water must become a lifestyle for you. It's not something you do over a period of a few months and then stop, otherwise as you already know, the results are temporary. If you commit to learning a new skill or starting a new business, then the process you follow next to achieve that goal MUST become a lifestyle for you.

Being successful at anything in life is not a one-time event, it's an ongoing endeavour.

I know I have repeated many of the phrases in this book quite a few times but, it repetition that gets things done. It's hearing the same things over and over again that get you to take action. It's doing the same actions over and over again that get the results you want.

The next few chapters will probably be the hardest to digest if you are not a person who is normally self-motivated or a go getter. These chapters are about all the missing ingredients that stop people from success in any endeavour. I'm going to mention things like,

"Early morning starts"

"Commitment"

"Persistence"

"Diligence"

"Planning"

"Rituals"

"Daily action"

"A game plan,"

All the things that are usually missing if you haven't already achieved the success you want.

Becoming successful means, you have to be prepared to start doing the things you haven't done before and the things that you won't feel like doing. Whether you want to hear it or not, being successful means getting up off your ass, not just once in a while when you feel motivated, but every single day and practically plugging your game plan into your life. Making things happen.

In the second part of this book we talked about visualisation and how powerful it can be when you use it on a regular basis. I am a huge believer in mind programming and the law of attraction principles. I truly believe it has an enormous effect on your success in life. I also believe where many people get it wrong (and I know this through experience working with many clients) is that they get caught up too much in the "thoughts become things" aspect of the process and don't take enough action on a daily basis to be successful. Nothing happens without action. It's the hard part, the part people avoid, the uncomfortable part, but it's the most important part.

When clients come to me for coaching, especially if they have been readers of "The Secret" or are followers of the "Law of Attraction Principles," I usually ask them a question which I borrowed from "Super Coach" author Michael Neill. When they hear the question I ask them to be totally honest with me. The question is this:

"If affirmations, visualisation and all that other mind stuff was all a load of crap, and the only way to get stuff was to practically get out there and do stuff, are you putting in the hours and taking enough action on a daily basis to get you to where you want to go?

And the answer I get more often than not is, No!

I have never met a successful person who hasn't put in consistent action and this involves a daily routine that consists of a set of rituals they put into place (which we will cover in the next chapter).

Mark's Story

Mark was a therapist and coach who came to me for help. He had been working in his profession for around five years and was in my opinion was pretty good at what he done. He had all the practical knowledge through years of reading and studying. When working with clients he was very successful at getting results. The problem was, he was scraping by and was barely earning a living from his profession. As we knew each other for a long time, I would usually see him every day and he would come to my clinic for a coffee or a chat and we discussed our day and how things were going. From Mark's stories I always seen a pattern in why he wasn't as busy as he would like to be but he was a great talker so I assumed he would sort things out. I usually threw small hints into our conversation as to how I would change things but didn't want to patronise him and tell him what I really thought. One day he came to me totally dismayed with himself and what he was doing and we had our usual coffee and a chat. He was on the verge of quitting. This time was different so I decided to pull no punches. I told him I was going to tell him "how it was" and hold nothing back. Mark's problem was that he wasn't a person of action. He talked about what he wanted to do and had loads of pointless meetings with people having coffee and talking nonsense about things that were irrelevant. He didn't market his services every single day, he didn't have a set of written goals and he didn't have a focus on one specific area of his coaching and therapy. He would always see someone doing well at a specific aspect of coaching or therapy and the next day he would jump into that for a week or so but generally never getting anything done. I think the term is "jack of all trades: master of none." He was always complaining about how there was no business out there and how bad the economy was and how no one was spending money and how where he lived was a bad area. I told him I was going to be totally honest and blunt with him and that I was. I started with telling him that if he kept doing what he was doing, he was going to end up stacking shelves in a supermarket or driving a taxi cab in a few months to bring in some money, which he didn't like at all but I think at some level he already knew that. I then asked him a series of questions that focused on kinds of action he had taken over the last seven days with his marketing, his goals list his time management and a few other things. He didn't have any of these things put into plan never mind taking action on them. He had no written goal list. He didn't advertise or market his services on social media sites at all, which was all free advertising. He didn't even have a list of services that he offered clients. He just relied on word of mouth advertising because someone told him that was the best, and sat waiting around for "The Universe" to bring him clients. Over the next few days we turned our coffee meetings into coaching sessions and I helped him develop a plan of action that he could take every day, that would help get himself out there, develop some new habits of getting up earlier and doing the basics to build himself a business rather than waiting on a miracle to happen. What I did with Mark was basic common sense. We got out a piece of paper and wrote down an action plan for him to put into place. I structured his day from when he got up in the morning (I had him get up three hours earlier every morning. His day usually started at 10am, I changed that to 7am) until he went to bed at night and all I asked from him was the commitment to follow through with this simple plan. That was just over a year ago. He did follow through and he's not stacking shelves at a supermarket or driving a taxi cab. He is now an action taker who is busier now in his therapy practice than he has ever been. Although we had to get him there kicking and screaming so to speak, this was what he really wanted and he adapted to change, taking deliberate action in no time at all.

I believe that being successful in anything in life is so simple and basic that it is overlooked. People get themselves involved in the grand scale of success, what they want and totally forget about the fundamentals that they need to put into place first to get them there.

We look at world champions in sport, see them in their hours of victory and we get caught up in wanting that. What we don't see is that same athlete getting up at 5am, going out and jogging in the rain, when it's cold and dark. We don't see that same athlete working in the gym at 10 pm on a Friday or Saturday night when everyone else is out partying and enjoying their weekend. We don't see that athlete disciplining their day so that they can get to that final stage.

We look at the successful businessmen in life, we admire their achievement and we get caught up in wanting that. What we don't see is that same man or woman getting up at 6am and coming home at maybe 10 or 11pm each day. We don't see the failures, the setbacks and the constant worry they go through, of maybe not being able to provide for their family. We don't see the discipline the people put in each day especially when nothing is going right. They take the daily action day after day in hard times when most people are relaxing and using their time unwisely. What you will find is that if you take the time to ask any of these successful men and women what the secrets of their success are, in all cases the answer that comes up the most is just turning up every day and taking deliberate action. It really is that simple. It's not an easy endeavour, by no means, but it is a simple one. It's the magic ingredient many people will avoid.

So let's develop a plan to help you succeed

"The path to success is to take massive, determined action."

(Tony Robbins)

11

Your Game Plan

"We stuck with our game plan and we got our results."

(Evgini Nabokov)

A game plan is a strategy that is worked out in advance for specific objectives. We hear of game plans for sporting events or election campaigns and usually they can be worked out down to the minute detail and when followed they usually produce the results that are written in advance. When things are not going to plan, as in a sporting game during the intervals, the game plan is adjusted to fit whatever obstacles come up along the way. Isn't your life more important than a game of sport? Yet I'm sure if I went out onto the street and asked one hundred people if they could tell me what their game plan was for their life, the majority of them would laugh at me and think I was some kind of a nut. Having a game plan will help you focus on where you are going, get into the daily habit of working your plan and getting to know if you are on track each day. So let's get started.

I want you to get out your journal. **You do have a journal by now, right?**

In your journal, I want you to bring up one of your goals (we will focus on one goal and you can replicate the procedure for the rest of your goals where needed).

Write the goal at the top of a blank page and we will start from there. Once you have your goal written down, you need to break that goal into monthly, weekly and daily chunks. When you have the goal broken down then all you have to do is simply focus on "today". You can't control next week. There's no point in worrying about next month because it's not here, so doesn't yet exist(remember). All you have is "today, so if you work on it, you start a process of developing your game plan, building a new habit and when the day comes to a close; you get out your journal, reflect on how you have done and what you have accomplished. You then tick off the small chunks you have achieved, give yourself a pat on the back and then before you go to sleep; plan tomorrow and write down a new set of projects you are going to work on, so that when you wake up tomorrow it is a new "today" and you can continue with your game plan as you did yesterday until the day is through and simply repeat the process.

When you get caught up in today, the days' pass, the weeks pass and you realise you have achieved what you wanted by implementing all the things that were missing in the past; things such as a game plan, discipline, consistence, habit, diligence and a review each night to make sure you are on track.

No magic formula, no luck or silver spoon involved, just basic common sense, a few simple applications each day and "YOU" taking responsibility for your life by consciously getting involved every day. You have started a system to make those goals a reality and you move onto the next, with the same strategy.

How to make your journal work for you?

The key to using your journal effectively is to plan your day the night before, by structuring what you will accomplish the next day.

When I first started structuring my day in this way I wrote myself a "to do" list each night and my aim was to go through the list and check off the tasks as I went through the day. The problem with this was that my lists just kept getting bigger and bigger. I would add more items as I went along and most of the time. I ended up with just as many uncompleted as I had completed when the day was over. I either added the uncompleted ones to the next day's list or just decided to go back to them again. This was counterproductive and caused more stress than it was worth, so I had to find a different approach by making a few simple adjustments. So I did.

I reframed what I was doing and I called it a **"must do list"**. The difference was that I made the process more achievable and set myself the task of completing between just four to six items maximum, each day. Instead of having twenty things to get through, I had maybe six and sometimes just four or five and I made these a must.

When something is a must, you make sure it's done. By lessening the amount of work and prioritising what I "must" get through each day, I was achieving a lot more and was less stressed when the day finished. I achieved everything I wanted to achieve each day and I finished off my days feeling good about myself.

A "Must do list" helps you build Confidence

Let me side track here for a moment. In my profession I would see a lot of people who come to me for lack of confidence. They want to do things, achieve things, accomplish things in their lives but in their mind they don't have the self-confidence to follow through.

When people come to me for more confidence, they are expecting a session full of affirmations and conscious techniques to help them become more confident, but this is how I see it.

Developing confidence is about having a structure in your life and doing simple things each day in a certain direction.

Self-confidence comes from doing the small daily disciplines each day in the direction of your goal. Self-confidence comes from feeling good about yourself and one of the best ways to feel good about yourself is, at the end of the day, knowing that you gave it your best. You practically achieve small steps each day in the direction of your goal. At the end of those days when you feel good about yourself because you have done what you said you were going to do, self-confidence starts to rise.

You know that if you can have one good day like this, you can have another one tomorrow and the next day and the next day and those days become weeks and the months become a powerful year.

Self-confidence comes from the lack of neglect of the small daily disciplines.

So when you are actively pursuing your dreams and not just talking about it, without action, self-confidence grows. You gain the confidence indirectly by the small successes you achieve each day.

Having a "must do list" and completing that list every day, will boost your confidence like nothing else.

So let us go back and break that down so I can show you an example of how you would do it step by step.

I deal a lot with weight loss in my practice so I will use this as my example.

Just to refresh from previous chapters; we think in pictures and what we habitually think is what has been programmed into our minds for years. The power words we use will have an effect on our psychology, remember.

So take the phrase, "Lose Weight." As children we have been programmed that when we lose something we are automatically programmed to do what? Go look for it. If you lose your phone or your car keys, you spend the next while looking for it. So the first thing I do with clients is to get them to forget about the word, "Lose" and replace it with the word "Release". When you release something you are letting it go. My clients make the decision to release the weight they no longer want and create an image in their mind of how they want to look instead. We then focus on the new image and associate the good feelings with this image. Then over a sustained period of time create a new concept of how to become your ideal weight, by mental rehearsal.

Goal: Become two stone lighter and become healthier in the process.

Game plan

How long will I take to release this amount of weight?

10 Weeks.

How can I break that two stone down into achievable chunks?

Two stone (28lbs) over ten weeks = 2.8lbs per week.

My new project is 2.8lbs per week over next ten weeks.

So let's break that down and develop a plan for each week.

What are the necessary steps I need to put into place for this process?

- Use a journal to plan my days and track my progress.
- Break down my eating into bite size chunks that will help me lose weight.
- Put a system into place each day that I can follow to make it easier to focus on today.

Let's go through an example step by step:

So in my journal it is Sunday evening and I have entered all the above information. My game plan starts tomorrow so I will plan each day the night before and reflect at the end of each day to make sure my game plan is on track.

Must Do List for Monday:

6am: (first thing I will do is weigh myself and record this in my journal as my starting weight. I will only weight myself once a week so that I can make sure I am on track).

6am: Two glasses of water then off to the gym for a workout

(Workout will last around one hour and thirty minutes)

8.30am: One full glass of water then Breakfast

10.30am: One full glass of water then two pieces of fruit

12pm: One full glass of water then lunch

2pm: One full glass of water then fruit or low fat yoghurt

5.30pm: One full glass of water then dinner

8pm One full glass of water then fruit or yoghurt

10pm: Before bed two full glasses of water

Journal entry and plan Tuesday.

Hypnosis audio based on my goals with positive content that will renew my mind and also help me wind down and switch off before I sleep (usually lasts twenty minutes).

I have made this very basic example simple to give you an idea of how the process goes. If I was doing this for real, I would obviously add what food I was going to have at each meal and I would make sure that each day the type of food changes so that there is plenty of variety in my daily eating plan.

The point here is that when I get up on Monday morning I have a game plan and I will stick to it throughout each day. I have a set of rituals that I will follow. If I get off track and eat a lot more in-between meals than I should have, then I will be totally honest and record this in my journal that night so I know where I went wrong on that day. If I weigh myself one week and I have not lost the weight I specified or even put on some weight, then I can go back to my journal and see what went wrong. If I go back and see that I over ate three or four times that week or maybe didn't follow my eating plan on a couple of the days, then I know what I have to adjust for the coming week.

What are my rituals in this example?

- Workout at 6am every day
- Glass of water before each meal
- Three meals a day
- Two light snacks in between each meal to help

overcome hunger
- Recording and planning in journal each night
- Hypnosis audio to help renew my mind and help me unwind and sleep better each night

If this was my goal I would implement these rituals every day, not just until the two stone is achieved but every day after that so that I maintain my ideal weight and this becomes a lifestyle for me. I know there will be times when I fall off track or decide to eat more than I should but if I have a plan of, I can record these in my journal and modify or adjust when I need to.

I have been involved in fitness and weight loss for a long time and I believe that this simple example above is the best way to lose weight and can be put into practice by anyone reading this book. Not only that, if you put this very system into practice and follow through then I guarantee you will lose weight; no diets, no forbidden foods, no calorie counting. Just basic common sense and following a daily set of rituals that you put in place the night before. Lots of water throughout the day to help the body flush itself out and help with elimination.

You need to develop a set of daily rituals that you are committed to. Willpower, as you know, only lasts for a certain amount of time but when you develop a set of rituals, putting them into place each day and this becomes a habit then these rituals become part of who you become. They shape your future by helping you build and structure each day. Remember all we have is today and when you are doing the right things today and every day, success becomes habit and that's what I call **"The Success Habit."**

The title of the book is called, "The Success habit: A Journey to Self-Mastery" which means doing the basic things every day, not only to help you become successful but helping you develop the person you need to become along the way, so that when you reach your goal, you're a totally different person; mentally, physically and emotionally.

When we think of the word "Mastery," we can be overwhelmed but it's simply repetition and habit. Anyone can become a master of something if they are willing to put in the hours and do the things necessary. A master of something is a person who is really good at what he or she does. Does this means that he never has a bad day or challenges or obstacles on a daily basis? No! It just means he is willing to do whatever necessary by re-adjusting his sails in times of challenges to develop a stronger Mind-Set. This can be achieved by anyone.

Daily rituals create mastery.

If you have a bad habit, then you already have a set of rituals that are contributing to that bad habit. It is the daily rituals you have put into place that make up that habit. We can have good or bad rituals and these will, when developed, will create a habit. Let's do an exercise on rituals: you will need your journal for this again.

I borrowed the next exercise from a Tony Robbins video many years ago and firstly used in on myself. Since then I have used it with my clients for over the last number of years because it gets amazing results, if you simply take the time to go through it and be totally honest with yourself.

Rituals Exercise

1) *Think of something you would like to really change in your life. Something that is important for you to change. A goal you have maybe written down earlier in your journal. Underneath this write down exactly where you are in achieving that goal. Remember tell it how it really is NOW. Be totally honest with yourself. E.g. goal maybe to lose weight but now I'm three stone over weight and have no motivation to get started.*

2) *Now write down what the rituals are that you have developed that are driving that old habit or behaviour. E.g. Four negative rituals driving an old weight habit could be, eating late at night, drinking four litres of cola each day, lying in bed instead of getting up and going to the gym and only eating one meal a day, at dinner time. These are all rituals. Be totally honest with yourself. Write down approximately ten things that you would consider rituals that you have, that are driving that old habit. There are a bunch of small rituals you are doing every day that are driving your behaviour. What are they?*

3) *Want is it you really want in this area of your life? If the goal was completed and you were there, what would that be? Be very specific here. e.g. my goal is to become my ideal weight which for me would be 11 stone, feeling totally fit and energetic each day, eating totally healthy and exercising*

every day. Once again be as specific as you can.

4) *What new rituals do you need to develop and put into place each day that will get you there? From you get up in the morning until you go to bed at night; what has to change? What would you need to do totally differently each day?*

Rituals are a way of saying I'm taking responsibility for my own success,

I'm steering my own ship and I will steer it with a set of revised rituals each day until that ship docks."

(Robert Herdman)

" I give myself very good advice, but I very seldom follow it."

(Lewis Carroll, Alice in Wonderland)

12

It's your Life: What Are You Going To Do About It?

"They might try to tell you how you can live your life, but don't forget it's your right to do whatever you like."

(Patrick Strump)

The reason you are the way you are in your life right now is because of the choices and the decisions you have made in the past. It has little to do with anything else. When the excuses are exhausted, the blame game no longer has the same sweetness about it and you reflect on why you are the way you are, the truth is that it's all down to you. So now that you have read through the content of this book, taken part in the exercises and taken inventory of a few things in your journal. You have a list of the things you want to achieve over the next number of years, so my question to you is this:

When clients come to me for help, after they have spent a

lot of time telling me about the things they don't want and what they would like to achieve, this is the question I always ask them and it is the question you should be asking yourself right now;

"What are you going to do about it?"

Getting what you want is all up to you. It's what you will decide to do or not do when you leave this book that will determine if you get what you want.

You're the boss, you're in control and what happens next is all down to you. You have to make the decision you are actually going to take whatever action is necessary to get started and follow through.

How many opportunities or years have you wasted in life because you put things off? When you decided you would do it tomorrow or Monday. Monday is a great day for procrastinators but they never specify which Monday, so it's great because there's no pressure, it could be any Monday.

Most people don't succeed because there's no urgency in their approach to life. There is no sense of "I must" do this today, it's usually always "oh I'll start tomorrow."

The thing is there are only so many tomorrows and then you look back and the years have passed. If you're serious about changing your life and achieving some of the goals you have listed while reading this book, you need urgency, you must start today. If not you're going to look back at your life and the only thing you will regret are the things you haven't done. You realise then you always had the potential and the ability to achieve every single one of them but what stopped you, was "YOU.".

So let me ask you that question once again with a twist:

"What are you going to do about it TODAY?"

You don't have to know everything about something to get started. You don't have to be great at something to succeed but you do have to get started to be successful. Getting started means taking the first step **TODAY.**

If you haven't got a journal by this stage get one, **TODAY.**

If you haven't started writing your goals, start **TODAY.**

If you want to start a new business, take that first step **TODAY.**

If you want to become your ideal weight, start a weight loss plan **TODAY.**

Whatever you want to become successful at take that, first step **TODAY.**

Make that decision **TODAY** to become a person of action and then over the next few weeks use the exercises and strategies in this book. See how many things you can achieve by developing a new set of rituals that you can put into place every single day taking the time at the end of each day to reflect in your journal on how you have done and what you need to adjust for tomorrow so that you remain on track. A pilot of an aircraft, on his journey from taking off to his final destination, is off course over 90% of the time but he can navigate and keep track of how he is doing by adjusting his course until he reaches his destination.

You're not going to get it right a hundred percent of the time but when you have a game plan and you execute that plan into your day, you are guaranteed to succeed. You don't even have to get it right every time. Nobody does.

Remember there is only one thing stopping you in your quest for being successful and that is you.

You can read as many books as you want but taking action is really the only way to get started. I know I have laboured this a bit but repetition is the mother of success and if you are told something often enough then it might just go in.

I have kept this book as straightforward as possible because I believe that success is a very simple process. When you go back to basics with just a few strategies then it works. As you get into some momentum and get going, you can update your knowledge and use different strategies to overcome obstacles along the way, help break through unconscious fears as you take bigger steps and learn new skills as you go along. To do this you have to get started first, keep things simple and workable and stick to the fundamentals every day.

If you only did one practical thing each day in the direction of your goals, after one week you have done seven new things, you have taken seven steps closer to your goal.

After one month you have taken thirty steps forward. If

you took thirty steps towards your goal how close would you be to achieving that goal. At the end of the year you would have taken over three hundred steps, given the fact you will have a few off days. And if you followed through for a full year, how many of those goals on your list would you have accomplished in the direction of your dreams in just one year?

Here's a great story on sticking with the basics and developing new habits.

The Paper Clip Strategy

In 1993, a bank in Abbotsford, Canada hired a 23-year-old stock broker named Trent Dyrsmid.

Dyrsmid was a rookie so nobody at the firm expected too much of his performance. Moreover, Abbotsford was still a relatively small suburb back then, tucked away in the shadow of nearby Vancouver, where most of the big business deals were being made. The first popular email services like AOL and Hotmail wouldn't arrive for another two or three years. Geography still played a large role in business success and Abbotsford wasn't exactly the home of blockbuster deals.

And yet, despite his disadvantages, Dyrsmid made immediate progress as a stock broker thanks to a simple and relentless habit that he used each day.
On his desk, he placed two jars. One was filled with one hundred and twenty paper clips. The other was empty. This is when the habit started.

"Every morning I would start with 120 paper clips in one jar and I would keep dialling the phone until I had moved them all to the second jar."
—Trent Dyrsmid

And that was it. One hundred and twenty calls per day. One paper clip at a time.

Within eighteen months, Dyrsmid's book of business grew to $5 million in assets. By age twenty-four, he was making $75,000. Within a few years, outside firms began recruiting him because of his success and he landed a $200,000 job with another company.

When he was asked about the details of his habit, Dyrsmid simply said, "I would start calling at 8 a.m. every day. I never looked at stock quotes or analyst research. I also never read the newspaper for the entire time. If the news was really important, it would find me from other ways. And that's all I did. I had a goal, I had a game plan for implementing that goal and I just did it every single day. It was that simple."

Dyrsmid is a great example of what I am trying to preach to you in this chapter; is that success is a result of committing to the fundamentals over and over again to develop good habits.

Visual Cues and how to use them.

The reason I believe Dyrsmid's strategy worked for him so

well is that he had a **"visual cue"** that was in front of him every day. Once he saw the jar it automatically triggered into his nervous system what he had to do.

Your journal is exactly the same. When you start your day the night before you know exactly what you have to do when you get up the next morning until you go to bed that night. You have already a game plan in place that you have pre-written and all you have to do is implement it and just repeat the same principle each day.

I would use visual cues every day and teach my clients to use them which they do with great success.

As well as your daily journal, you can add many other visual cues to your daily routine. The simplest form is small "post its" with your goal or affirmation written on it and placed somewhere you will see it when you get up each morning, i.e. the mirror in your bedroom or bathroom or somewhere in the kitchen. The key is putting them somewhere you will be as soon as you awaken. Once you get out of bed the visual cue will remind you of your goal or what you need to do.

When you set a goal it is great to have a picture of that goal somewhere. You will see it every day to remind you of "Why" you are striving so hard. This is so important, especially in hard times when you're are struggling and you need that instant motivation.

When I feel I need to release some weight, I start implementing a certain eating program that I have been using for years which always works for me. I know what my meals will be, I have a variation so that I don't get bored with the same old foods and I know what times I will eat at each day. I also use a great visual cue that really helps me when I am feeling a bit "munchy," as I call it, which usually happens at night (sound familiar). On an A5 sheet of paper I have written, in permanent black marker,

"DO YOU REALLY WANT REACH THE IDEAL WEIGHT YOU PROMISED YOURSELF: OR WILL YOU JUST OPEN THIS FRIDGE AND EAT CRAP YOU DON'T EVEN WANT, JUST LIKE EVERYONE ELSE WOULD DO?"

I put this on the outside of my fridge door so it's right there when I'm tempted to reach for extra food I don't need.

This plays on the emotions and usually triggers the old guilt feeling so it stops me, rather than eating a bunch of food and feeling the guilt afterwards.

As you go through this system you will develop your own rituals and habits that will aid in your success.

I have a list of goals in my journal and what I have done is taken 1 page for each goal. I write the goal on the top of the page and a timescale of when I will achieve this goal. I then have a picture of the goal printed out from my computer and stuck to the other side of the page so that when I am writing up my "Must Do List" each day, I can go back and look at all my goals. Not only going over the goals but seeing the goal visually on the back of each page is a very powerful way for me to visualise myself achieving that goal. I keep everything in the one place (my journal) so that I am developing a habit of renewing, reviewing and keeping myself self-motivated each day. Visual cues can benefit you in many ways. They can help you:

- Start a new behaviour through a reminder each morning.
- Help keep you motivated on a daily basis.
- Help you to develop a new habit.

My purpose in this book is to help you to develop new habits because when you develop new habits you will become successful. If you think about it, the only thing that is stopping you from becoming successful at the moment is your bad habits.

In the story above Trent Dyrsmid decided that success in his field came down to one core task; making more sales calls. He discovered that mastering the fundamentals is what makes the difference.

The same is true for your success in life, no matter what success means to you. There is no magic secret. There is no secret recipe. Developing good habits is the secret.

The difference between successful people and people who just get by in life is the difference in their habits. Successful people develop good habits and unsuccessful people develop bad habits, both live by those habits on a daily basis. Ninety percent of what we do is through our unconscious, its habit; habitual thought patterns, habitual behaviours, habitual limiting beliefs, habitual negative programming. You create a habit and then in a short space of time, that habit creates you. The interesting thing about all habits is that they can be changed, it doesn't matter how old you are or how young you are. It doesn't matter if you've have been doing it for years, once you have reached the stage where you are sick and tired of being sick and tired and you have that willingness and desire for success, you can start the process of developing new habits in the direction of your goals. Instead of taking the time to do what is necessary and develop the fundamentals, most people will make excuses and do everything in their power to stay the same and it's never their fault. They all have their story of why they are the way they are. Well if this is you, you have only two options; either just keep doing what you're doing or make a "Quality Decision" to change. Decide that enough is enough and you have the right to be successful, just like any other successful person on the planet. You will step up, walk the walk and become a person of action. Like Nike says, "Just Do It."

"Everything you need is already within you. The beauty of life is that your DESTINY lies always within your hands. The time has come for you to Step UP and BE GREAT."

(PABLO)

13

Step Up or Shut Up!

"The universe doesn't give you what you ask for with your thoughts, it gives you what you DEMAND with your actions."

(Dr. Steve Maraboli)

So I have come to the final chapter in this journey. This book has been a journey for me that has taken around two years. Not because it has taken me two solid years to write but it has taken me two years, from I started it, until getting it completed. Everything I have mentioned in this book held me back.

- I put it off and put it off.
- I made all the excuses.
- I didn't take the action required.
- I let other people's opinion cloud my judgment.
- I didn't think I was good enough to write and have a published book.
- I was simply procrastinating most of the time.

I have come a long way in my journey in life and I have so much more that I will achieve in this new adventure which I find myself on right now. I'm not the person I used to be way back once upon a time and my beliefs have totally changed as to who I am and what I can achieve in life. The one key factor that changed for me was that **I started to believe in ME.** In getting this book completed, there was one other specific event that happened to me that really gave me a kick up the ass. It got me motivated to get this done and I want to share it with you before we get into this final chapter.

Robert's book story

It was just a normal day in my Hypnotherapy practice. I had full days' worth of clients booked in and I went through the day as I usually did; giving the best of myself in each session and helping as best as I could to help turn people's lives around. I love what I do and every day is totally different, so it's not really work to me but a passion I dive into every day. I had one client left before the day finished who was coming to me for some coaching. He was a regular client that I had seen over a period of about a month and he had made some amazing progress in his professional career as a MMA fighter and in his personal life, dealing with day to day issues that used to get him down and detracted from his goals. We had worked together on his Mind-Set and his game plan for his career and I had done my bit, helping him turn things around. After the session, we had a cuppa (anyone who knows me will know I'm a tea fanatic) and he asked me what my goals were. We chatted and I told him about writing my book. "Ah the famous book," he replied and started laughing. I was a bit pissed at his reaction, which I thought quite arrogant, as I had never mentioned the book to him before, but he was a cage fighter remember, so I analysed the situation in my head very carefully, pretending his comments didn't faze me. I acted cool and asked him to explain his comments. He was recommended to me by a few other fighters who I had worked with from the same gym and they had told him to ask me about this famous book. One of my main goals from when I started in personal development was to write a book and I had the tendency to go on about it without ever putting it into practice (sound familiar). So as I had worked with a few of his comrades they had all heard about the "famous book" that never was. He had explained this and as he finished he said to me, "Well I suppose it would be time to step up or shut up." This was a trigger they used in the gym with all their fighters before they entered into the ring, to give them a bit of a kick and it totally worked for me.

When he left my office, my attitude was, "that's it, I will show them," and immediately within five minutes was on the computer, planning out the chapter content of this "famous book."

So I throw that same challenge out to you as we come to the end of this book together. It's time to **"Step up or Shut up".** If you really want to become successful in a certain area of your life, you have to make a start sometime. There are only so many tomorrows and you are running out of time, so why not make that start today, and I mean today, when you have finished reading. Do one thing that could start you off in the new direction towards achieving some of those goals that you put into your journal. **You have started a journal, right?**

Go back to basics and start with the fundamentals. Become like a fighter in training every day; developing yourself mentally and physically on the way to your goals. You need to; it's a must if you want success to last. You need to become a different person than you are right now and that starts with developing yourself.

I have enjoyed the experience of writing this book and my goal for 2016 is to write and publish two more books so watch this space. The next is already in the making.

I do hope I have helped some people along the way by simplifying things so that some of you feel that you are equipped to actually go out, put some of this information into practice and achieve your goals.

We live in what I call a "microwave world" today and everything seems to be rush, rush, rush, meaning that people are more stressed now than ever. Remember that the principles of success should be a simple process, making the decision to take responsibility for your own life, setting out a game plan and sticking to the mechanics of that game plan each day. Making the effort to continually revise what you are doing along the way so that you know you are still on track.

If you decide to be one of the small percentage of people who leave this book and start a new journey of going for your goals, the road ahead is going to be paved with obstacles, hurdles, setbacks, failures. You will probably have the negative opinions of other people trying to put you off. You are also going to come against hard times when you will need the ability to dig deep within yourself and summon all your resources to carry you through the rough times. You will have that little voice inside your head telling you to quit but this is where part two of this book will stick by you, if you actually take the time to renew your mind.

When you go through the process of renewing your mind, what you are doing is programming your mind with new material that will come out when you need it.

I have had some really challenging times in my journey over the last ten years where I actually thought I was possessed or going insane. It was as if the battle within my mind was so strong, I thought I was losing the plot. By implementing all the material I have shared with you in this book I was able to, **"Keep Moving Forward"** and I did what had to be done.

When I was at the stage where I was stressed and wasn't making good decisions, I stopped what I was doing and I took fifteen to twenty minutes to myself. If I needed more time, I took the day off and I did something totally different that didn't involve work so that my mind could unwind and I came back the next day with a better perspective. Each day I made sure that I got into the habit of taking time for myself. This started with ten minutes and now as I write this material I take twenty minutes each day to renew mind, in the morning when I awaken. This helps me start each day with a positive Mind-Set and this in itself, has totally transformed my entire life.

Remember there is a price to pay for everything in life and you have to decide by making a "Quality Decision" to do whatever it takes, no matter what, to achieve the success you want. Now for some of you reading this, that success could mean something really small that you have been striving for but for others it could mean a life change or a career change. No matter what it is, you have to be prepared to deal with the bad times as well as the good instead of moaning and feeling sorry for yourself, find a way to take that step forward each time.

Let me share with you one final story.

I had been in private practice as a Clinical Hypnotherapist for just over two years and things were going great for me. I had learnt so much, helped so many people and I was earning really good money doing what I really loved doing. After all these years, I was finally happy and contented in something I knew was my passion and hopefully something I would be involved with for the rest of my life. I had developed a five-year plan and had ideas of developing my own audio online programs that people could purchase throughout the world, my own online coaching program and a corporate training program where I could go into companies and show people how to develop their Mind-Set. I knew what I wanted to do for the next ten years and this excited me. But then the economy took a downturn and the world was turned upside down. The news was filled with scare stories of banks falling apart and the word, "credit crunch," was everywhere. People lost millions on property investments and people stop spending. My business, like every other business at that time, started to feel the strain. I got loads of cancellations to start off with and as the months moved forward I got less and less clients. I was renting an office in the centre of Belfast city which was expensive so I was getting things tight financially. I made the decision to look for a smaller office outside the city, which I found, and moved premises into a smaller village on the outskirts but still close enough for people to travel. But things never improved. I blamed the people, I blamed the economy, I cursed the banks, like everyone else did, and I got involved in the herd mentality again of why things were going wrong. People started giving me their best advice, "quit while you're ahead", "get yourself a job," all the usual. I felt totally dismayed to say the least, I was doing what I loved and I didn't want to get a normal job. But then my couple of years of mental training started to kick in. I started to ask myself better questions. I got out my journal at that time and wrote down all the possibilities of how I could move forward and most of them weren't good. I was even offered a job by a friend who owned a restaurant but I knew if I took that job that would be it. I would be pulled away from my own Mind-Set and get comfortable with the regular wage. My pride was eating away at me, after all I was the Hypnotist who had a successful business and I would be the laughing stock of everyone I knew; from Hypnotist to waiter and bartender. My mind went crazy again and that little storyteller inside my head was let loose making up all sorts of nonsense as it went along. I decided to take a couple of days off with the intention that something would come to me. There was no way in hell I was giving up my dream but I needed money fast so I had to come up with a better alternative

The other problem was that Christmas was close by and I had to get my income active again because with everything that happened over the previous few months, I was almost broke.

I was sitting reading the local paper, something I would never do normally, and I saw an advert that said, "part-time door to door leaflet delivery people wanted for Christmas: Paid Weekly." I looked at this advert and read what was involved. It was going door to door putting leaflets through letterboxes advertising local businesses, discounting their services and products. I made the decision to swallow my pride and enquired about the job but I had an ulterior motive if I got the position.

Well I did get the job and I was to start after the weekend. The company were doing huge leaflet drops throughout Northern Ireland so you were able to pick the area you wanted to work. I decided to pick an area outside of Belfast where no one knew me so I didn't

meet anyone that could point the finger with the "told you so" speech.
I had a cunning plan that made this idea work for me, helped me not
to be hard on myself and helped me not to think of this as a failure.
This was a stepping stone, so I had to make the most of it. What I
did next I would say actually saved my business and helped me
continue to have a small but steady flow of hypnotherapy clients while
I was taking care of my finances.

On the Thursday before I was to start I got onto my computer and I
designed three separate hypnotherapy flyers; one for weight loss, one for
stress and anxiety and one for the new year, new goals. I went to my
local printer and I got him to print out ten thousand flyers and kept
them in the trunk of my car. On Monday morning I went and picked
up the leaflets I was to deliver for this new company and I set out to
my destination to distribute them. I added my own flyers to the pack
and armed each day with Zig Ziglar, Tony Robbins and Jim Rohn
on my iPod, I worked around seven hours each day, delivering leaflets
through doors, making a steady income but all the while promoting
my own business. After the first week, my office phone started to ring
and I only took evening clients as I told clients I was fully booked
each day. My clientele started to become more frequent and over a
short period of time I was able to rebuild my business again. I moved
office once again back into the city but at a less expensive place and I
haven't looked back since.

I delivered leaflets for about six weeks but each day I was listening to
my iPod, renewing my mind, self-motivating and getting my own offers
in front of people at the same time. I was getting fit with all that
walking so I was achieving quite a lot when you think about it.
When I set up my Hypnotherapy practice in 2007 I didn't have a
plan B if it all went wrong, because I didn't want a plan B. I was
prepared to do whatever it took to succeed and I have learnt
sometimes that means doing things you don't want to do in the short
term so that you can get to where you want to be. When you are in
business you can't afford to let your pride take over, you have to learn
to, "swallow your pride and: keep moving forward" remember.

I want to thank you for your time and hope that it was of some value. I hope I have been of some assistance in helping you develop some structure that you can implement in becoming successful.

I have lots to share with you that I have learned over the last ten years. Helping you continue the process of developing yourself from the inside out so that the success on the outside can be achieved with less stress, more enjoyment and as easily as possible, but that is for another book and another journey. So I wish you every success in whatever success means to you and remember that probably the most important thing I can leave you with is that you need to leave this book and take action. I don't mean once in a while but every day. Become a person of action and if you haven't already done so, start that first action step and, **"Go and Buy a Bloody Journal"**

I wish you every success in your new journey, should you make the effort to start one, and I hope I have been a mere spark in the start of that journey and until next time I leave you with this Irish blessing:

May the road rise to meet you.
May the wind be always at your back.
May the sun shine warm upon your face.
And rains fall soft upon your fields.
And until we meet again,
May God hold you in the hollow of his hand.

Don't Quit

When things go wrong, as they sometimes will,

When the road you're trudging seems all uphill,
When the funds are low and the debts are high,
And you want to smile, but you have to sigh,
When care is pressing you down a bit-
Rest if you must, but don't you quit.

Life is queer with its twists and turns,

As every one of us sometimes learns,
And many a fellow turns about
When he might have won had he stuck it out.
Don't give up though the pace seems slow -
You may succeed with another blow.

Often the goal is nearer than

It seems to a faint and faltering man;
Often the struggler has given up
When he might have captured the victor's cup;
And he learned too late when the night came down,
How close he was to the golden crown.

Success is failure turned inside out -

The silver tint in the clouds of doubt,
And you never can tell how close you are,
It might be near when it seems afar;
So stick to the fight when you're hardest hit -
It's when things seem worst that you must not quit.

Recommended Reading List

To help you on your journey to success I will list a few of the many books that have had a great effect on my life.

I have used these authors as my mentors throughout the years and I have studied with some of them personally. Others I have read, re-read and digested their material and implemented it into my life and the lives of my clients.

Being successful at anything is not about re-inventing the wheel. It's about taking a proven system or set of principles that have worked time and time again and practically and emotional plugging them into your life.

I cannot possibly list all the material I have read over the years but I feel this short reading list, if acted upon and digested, will get you started and start the process of transforming anyone's life.

The Secret Language of Feelings: Cal Banyan.

You Can Have What You Want; Michael Neill.

Super Coach; Michael Neill.

7 Strategies for Wealth and Happiness; Jim Rohn.

The Five Major Pieces to the Life Puzzle; Jim Rohn.

Unlimited Power; Anthony Robbins.

Awaken the Giant Within; Anthony Robbins.

Make Your Life Great; Richard Bandler.

Get the Life You Want; Richard Bandler.

The Law of Success; Napoleon Hill.

Think and Grow Rich; Napoleon Hill.

Born to Win; Zig Ziglar.

See You at the Top; Zig Ziglar.

No Excuses: The Power of Self Discipline; Brian Tracy

Maximum Achievement; Brian Tracy.

The Power of Your Sub-conscious mind; Dr. Joseph Murphy.

The Richest Man in Babylon; George S Clason.

The Alchemist; Panlo Coelho.

Change Your Life in 7 Days; Paul McKenna.

"Every story has an end,

But in life, every end is simply a new beginning

Start your new story of how you became successful

Go make things happen for You"

(Robert Herdman)

Until we meet again, Every Success and God Bless

Robert

About the Author

Robert Herdman has been a (NGH) Certified Clinical Hypnotherapist since 2007. He has a busy full time private practice in Belfast, Northern Ireland where he spends his time teaching people how to enhance their lives. Over the last ten years he has travelled throughout the world updating his knowledge base and has accumulated the skills needed, to help over ten thousand clients both on a one to one basis and through his workshops and seminars lead a more fulfilling life. He is also a licensed Master Practitioner in Neuro Linguistic Programming and Success Coach. As well as working with clients on an individual basis he has just embarked on a new journey as a Keynote Speaker. He teaches groups and companies the mechanics behind "The Success Habit," showing them a way to become more productive by developing the Mind-Set of their workforce.